GOOD HOUSEKEEPING
Book of Wine

Book Club Associates
London

This edition published 1974 by
Book Club Associates
by arrangement with
Ebury Press

Line drawings by Chris Evans
Photographs Plates 2 and 3 by Dennis Hughes-Gilbey,
remaining plates by Percy Hennell

For their help with the preparation of this book, GOOD
HOUSEKEEPING would like to thank the following:
Food From France; Deinhard & Co.; González Byass
Ltd; Grierson-Blumenthal Ltd; J. L. P. Lebègue & Co.
Ltd, and Rutherford, Osborne & Perkin Ltd.

EDITED BY JO NORTHEY

Filmset and printed in Great Britain by
BAS Printers Limited, Wallop, Hampshire
and bound by
G & J Kitcat Ltd, Shand Street, London SE1

Contents

Colour Plates

Illustrations in Text

Part One

A Guide to Understanding Wine

Chapter 1 *The Wonder of Wine*

Wine is one of the oldest pleasures of life. No one knows exactly when it was discovered, but probably it was first made when some juice pressed from freshly-gathered grapes was forgotten, fermented by itself, and later someone found how delicious the subsequent drink could be.

All around the Mediterranean, the cradle of civilization as it has rightly been called, the grape vine flourished, often in places where no other crop except the hardy olive tree grew, and the fermented juice of the grape, as well as the actual fruit, came to be valued and cultivated.

In many religious rituals recorded thousands of years before Christ, wine played an important part, and it was revered and respected because of its stimulating properties. In classical times, the wine drunk in certain religious ceremonials acted as a means of liberating those participating from their cares and inhibitions – these occasions sometimes turned into what might be described as an orgy, but originally wine was intended to liberate the spirit from care and prepare the personality for the reception of the god being worshipped.

Another reason why wine was prized was as a disinfectant, one of the earliest known to man. Water from a doubtful source of supply could be rendered comparatively harmless by the addition of a little wine; food was washed in wine or vinegar to clean it and keep it wholesome in the days before refrigeration and, as the parable of the Good Samaritan recounts, wounds were washed with wine to combat risk of infection and then dressed with oil to soothe them.

The reference by St Paul to take 'a little wine for thy stomach's sake' indicates how anyone in poor health, needing a slight stimulant, something to create an appetite or by way of a digestive, could take wine, often mixed with water or rendered even more medicinal with herbs and spices, both as a preventative and a cure.

Today, many doctors recommend the use of wine as an adjunct to food because it is, in fact, a food as well as a drink and can also be an admirable digestive. Its gentle stimulation can encourage anyone with a jaded appetite to approach a meal with enthusiasm and digest it well. Very often a glass of wine is recommended as part of a diet for convalescents, and also as a means of relaxing tension in anyone who has been under strain, so that he can enjoy food more easily.

More than this, though, wine is possibly the supreme convenience food. Not only does it enhance the enjoyment of food and help the digestion of the diner, but it can transform a very ordinary snack or pot-luck dish into something special for offering without a moment's hesitation to the unexpected guest, however eminent. Even the simplest family fare can be fit for 'company' with a well chosen bottle of wine, and this need not be expensive.

Indeed, even a bottle of cheap wine can save the day with a meal planned at short notice because, whereas accidents can always happen to the food, the wine is far less likely to let you down; and if it does, the fault is not yours, so you needn't be ashamed of saying that it isn't as good as you wish; then your guests can criticize it too. Talking about and even criticizing a wine can be fun so long as there is no reflection on the hospitality of host or hostess.

The home 'cellar' that consists of only a single bottle arms you against the unexpected guest, the unforeseen celebration, and even consolation. There is nothing very time-consuming about opening a bottle, after all.

Wine and the world we live in   Sharing wine has always been an important part of hospitality in wine-drinking countries and, to a lesser degree, echoes the fellowship implied by the ritual of sharing wine in many religious ceremonies. Its stimulating effect makes people more easy-going and willing to talk to each other, even if they are shy, and if all else fails they can always talk about the wine!

The respect which wine has always enjoyed as a health-giving and sometimes a semi-sacred commodity has caused it to be surrounded by many conventions; some are based on sound commonsense to do with its selection and service, others are merely the expression of fashions or customs that by now may be many years, even centuries, out of date.

There is no reason for anyone to be intimidated by the mystique that has grown up around wine, although there is a definite mystery to it. Wine is a wonderful thing, capable of giving great enjoyment and possessing many properties which might well have seemed magical to our ancestors; but first and foremost, it is a drink to be enjoyed, and this should never be forgotten.

The only conventions that are worth considering and following are those that increase the enjoyment of the drinker. There are only a few of these – someone once said that all the essentials the would-be wine drinker needs to know can be written on the back of a postcard – and they are simple to understand.

The knowledge gained by talking to people and their interchange of opinions are among the most civilizing aspects of life; today, national boundaries are more in the nature of challenges to the adventurous rather than barriers, and people are able to travel, both for pleasure and business, to an extent unparalleled in the past. There is no greater compliment to pay a visitor than to share hospitality, and there is no quicker way of learning what people are really like than by getting to know them around a dinner table.

Wine that you may have enjoyed in a restaurant on some special occasion or that reminds you of a holiday abroad can also enhance your own entertaining, because on sale in Britain today there is a range of the wines of the world, unparalleled in any other country. Getting to know some of these wines is something which your friends will surely be interested in sharing with you.

Wine is a hallmark of civilized company and anyone entertaining for business purposes, both in restaurants or at home, will find wine a most valuable asset. You will find that a little wine know-how can reap rewards out of all proportion to the time it takes to learn the basics of this intriguing subject. And the enjoyment that even simple wines can bring will definitely be out of all proportion to their cost.

People are often nervous of learning about wine because they are under the impression that it is difficult, but nothing is further from the truth. No one can know everything about wine, but everyone can know something. Even the greatest authorities on wines are always learning, and the truly great among them are never bored by a sincere question from a beginner, or by an honest comment.

The fascinating thing about wine is that it can exercise the intelligence as well as the senses, and that's why people who are genuinely interested in learning about wine are usually people of lively minds and humble hearts! Everyone in the world of the wine lover learns every day and all the time.

Another reason why people are hesitant about wine is the popular belief that it is a 'man's world'. It is strange that this view is still held by anyone, because wine is bought increasingly by women who in fact buy more than men. It is, therefore, only sensible shopping if women know something about a commodity on which they are spending their money. Men, as a moment's reflection will confirm, have to start learning about wine as well – they're not born with knowledge of it! Maybe it is easier for a man to gain some experience of wine drinking, simply because in business he gets more opportunity to do so, but now that most women have a job before marriage and then continue to work afterwards, at least for part of the time, and when people in all walks of life travel extensively, it's not so difficult to get experience of wine.

Only Britain upholds the view that wine is for men only; certainly in the wine regions of the world there are women whose knowledge of wine has won the respect of many producers. There are many women who direct great estates and who are active in the wine trade, both in Britain and abroad, and very respected members of the wine trade are definite that they enjoy tasting wine in the company of a woman because, they say, 'women have no preconceived ideas, make up their own minds, and speak about the wines exactly as they find them'.

Indeed, women may start with an advantage over men. Taste is very largely a matter of smell, and a woman's experience in preparing and cooking food keeps her alerted to smells, both good and bad, and to taste. So there is really no reason at all why a woman should ever leave the choice of wine to the man and, because she most likely has to go and shop for the bottle, she would be wise to know what is involved.

The wine snob Out of the mystique about wine has emerged the wine snob, a stupid person whose misguided actions do more harm than good to the image of wine. One type of wine snob, who behaves in an unnecessarily showy way, is almost certainly someone who knows little or nothing about wine – the sort of person who is said 'to drink the label', in other words, drink only expensive or showy wines which have been talked about. The pretentious way in which such people approach a glass of wine – holding it up to the light, sniffing it as if it were Friar's Balsam, making faces as it is taken into the mouth and, finally, uttering a lot of high-flown statements which mean very little if anything at all – is rightly the subject of ridicule. No one who really cares about wine would do any of these things.

The true lover of wine will be far more interested in whether it is enjoyable or not, regardless of price, pedigree or the pretty picture on the label.

There is another type of snobbery, equally to be avoided. In a reaction against the pretentious language and affected ways of people who style themselves 'experts' or 'connoisseurs', this wine snob goes to the other extreme; he treats all wines alike, refusing to admit that there are degrees of quality, and doesn't bother with even the most elementary observances of service, which make wine enjoyable. This is the kind of person who will make a point of serving tepid white wine, something very expensive perhaps in a coloured plastic beaker, or taking a fine red wine on a picnic, or serving what is really a picnic wine at a dinner party on which every amount of care and expense has otherwise been lavished, and say thoughtlessly that 'it is all the same really'.

Absence of care is as misguided as too much and both types of snobbery can give great offence to others. However, there's no need to be concerned with them any further, and in any case, wine snobs are really interested only in themselves.

The facts about wine

People have written pages of very purple prose and uttered impassioned speeches about the wonder of wine. Certainly it is beautiful and mysterious, but its creation is also something that happens as a result of natural and chemical processes. Defining it is rather like trying to define a baby, a flower, or a happy marriage – the purely factual definition misses out the wonder and the mystery, while elaborate and poetic descriptions omit the facts and the chemistry. Ideally, the two should be combined.

What is wine? Let's start with the definition of wine as given by the Wine and Spirit Association of Great Britain. This says that 'wine is the alcoholic beverage obtained from the juice of freshly-gathered grapes, the fermentation of which has been carried through in the district of its origin and according to local tradition and practice'. This is not really difficult to understand if the different things to which it refers are considered separately.

First, wine is made only from grapes, not any other fruits, berries or vegetables. These grapes must be freshly gathered, which means that wine cannot be made from dried grapes which are later reconstituted and made into an alcholic beverage, nor can wine be made by the addition of yeasts to imported or reconstituted grape juice to convert it into an alcoholic beverage. The drink made by any of these processes may be pleasant and perfectly acceptable, as well as commercially big business, but it cannot strictly be called wine. The grapes must be freshly gathered, therefore, and allowed to ferment where they are gathered, according to the custom of that particular place – by which is implied a wine-producing region.

Fermentation The process of fermentation may sound complicated in terms of chemistry, but anyone who can understand enough to cook can understand fermentation, which is simply the conversion of the sugar contained in the grapes into alcohol.

This conversion is carried out by the action of the wine yeasts, which work upon the unfermented grape juice (known as must) just as yeasts work in bread-making. The yeasts need sugar to do their work and grape juice is high in natural sugar. They also need a reasonably high temperature or else they cannot get to work, but the temperature must neither rise too high nor drop too low so that they cease to work. They should do their work naturally and quickly, and this is why the time of the vintage, when the grapes are gathered and made into wine, is one of great excitement and, in certain years, of anxiety because the process of fermentation may be handicapped by sudden rises or falls in temperature, just as the baking of bread is hindered if there is a sudden draft or the temperature where the dough is proving suddenly goes up.

The process of fermentation can take a few days or even weeks, because it varies according to the type of wine and where it is being made. Usually it begins soon after the grapes are gathered, which is in the autumn in the northern hemisphere, while in the southern hemisphere, such as in South Africa or Australia, it begins in what is our spring.

The fermentation dies down or stops altogether when the temperature drops at the beginning of winter, but usually it starts again in the following spring; this second fermentation is the last stage in the making of wine as a finished product. Once it has taken place, the wine is then either bottled shortly afterwards or, with wines that gain in quality if they are allowed to mature for some time before going into bottle, it will rest and develop usually in cask. Wines that are actually undergoing fermentation are inclined to be slightly fizzy and may taste quite unlike their finished selves; sometimes they have what people describe as a 'beery' taste, and they certainly should not be drunk while they are in this condition because even a slight fermentation in wine may continue inside the drinker, rather like a dose of salts, with uncomfortable results.

Life cycle of the vine So how wine is made is, therefore, a comparatively simple process. But all sorts of fascinating things take place during this process; for example, the fact that the vintage usually starts exactly 100 days after the vine has flowered in the spring. This flowering is, after the vintage itself, the most important period in the life of the vine, and bad weather or lack of careful tending of the vineyard can have a lasting bad effect on the vine itself. The flowers on the vine are tiny and barely perceptible unless you are looking for them, but the slight fragrance given off a vineyard during the flowering period is delicate and quite unmistakable.

There is another wonderful thing about the cycle of a vine's life and its bearing on wine. Both at the time of the flowering of the vine in the spring and again at the time of the vintage in the autumn, many wines already in bottle (some of them may have been bottled for many years) tend to be a little unreliable; sometimes they are less than at their best, sometimes slightly disappointing, but generally they are unsettled. It seems as if there is some mysterious but definite tie between the vines and the wine for the whole of its life, so that at the time of spring and autumn equinoxes it pays to remember the season and be a little indulgent to a wine that might otherwise come in for severe criticism. However, not all wine is adversely affected by this link between the vine and the wine in bottle, but it is something that can happen.

Throughout the year, care of the vineyard is necessary as with any crop: it has to be weeded, protected from pests by spraying, the vines have to be

A special tractor
designed to straddle
the rows of vines

pruned so that they give a good yield and, when the vinestocks become too
old to fruit profitably, they are pulled up, the land rested, and young vines
planted in their place. Anyone with a garden will immediately understand
the cycle of events in a vineyard and something of the work involved. It goes
on the whole year round, and much of the cultivation has to be done by hand,
even in these days when as many processes as possible are mechanised.

Aspect of the
vineyard

Another interesting point about vineyards is that the vine shares with the
olive the ability to flourish in soils and in climates where no other crops will
grow and where the vine itself often has to fight to survive. Indeed, many of
the finest wines of the world come from vineyards which are positively bleak
and barren: for example, in the vineyards of the Upper Douro where port
comes from, the soil is so stony, consisting of granite chips, that the vines
can only be planted by blasting holes in which to put them. In many vineyards the extreme heat of the sun is almost unbearable in the summer,
whereas in the winter violent storms and winds can batter the vineyards,
as in parts of the Rhône valley. It is not unknown for an entire grape
harvest to be destroyed in a matter of minutes because of a sudden hailstorm.
Snow can lie thick on northern vineyards and some wines are made from
grapes which are actually frozen, such as the 'ice wines' of Germany.

It is one of the wonders of wine that the vine survives such conditions, and it is a greater wonder that the greatest wines come from regions where it would seem everything was against the vine and its bearing grapes for wine-making. It is rather like a person, subjected to hard conditions and opposition from all sides, who determines to succeed in spite of all obstacles. It is this curious circumstance which means that a rich soil, where other crops grow happily, is not usually good in vineyards that are going to produce very fine wines; medium quality and pleasant wine may be produced there, but nothing outstanding.

There are many different wines, and, whereas some wines are made from a single grape variety, others will contain a mixture of several different kinds of grapes, sometimes both red and white being used together. But, in general, red wines are made from red grapes, which are usually referred to as black grapes, and white wines from white grapes.

The way the vines grow varies too; some are trained straight up, to about the height of a human being, others are trained very low, extending along wires, so that vintagers have to stoop low to pick the grapes; some vines are grown on gently undulating slopes, others on steeply terraced hillsides. In each wine region the growers have evolved methods of cultivation that they have found most satisfactory. To a wine lover the sight of a well-kept vine-yard is beautiful and exciting, but it is only fair to say that it is, after all, only another agricultural crop, and if you are not likely to be excited by a field of wheat or potatoes in prime condition, then an endless vista of vines will probably not seem very thrilling either.

The vintage When the grapes on the vines are perfectly ripe they are picked, and this is known as the vintage. It takes place in the autumn from about the middle of September, as far as the South of Spain, Portugal and Southern Italy are concerned, and beginning a little later as one travels north, so that the vintage in Champagne will probably begin about the end of September or in October, and in the German vineyards it may not begin until late October or even November. Grapes are still harvested by hand, but the use of mechanical harvesters is growing, particularly in North America.

Bands of pickers start out early in the day and work through the vineyards, their task being extremely hard – especially under the blaze of a hot sun; people who think of earning a little pin-money by doing a few hours light work in a vineyard should ask themselves whether they would be good at lifting potatoes with the temperature well above 24°C (75°F)!

Once the grapes are ripe, they must be harvested quickly, and they usually seem to grow either high up so that vintagers have to stretch for them or low down so that they are bent double all day long. Of course, there's a good deal of fun had by the harvesters but the work is hard and long.

Pruning vines in
readiness for
the spring

Although there is usually a party when the vintage is over, this is by no means the sort of elegant affair that is portrayed in musical comedies or artists' impressions of vintage scenes from centuries past!

Pressing the grapes
In order to make wine the juice has to be extracted from the grapes. In the past, this was usually done either by pressing the grapes with enormous presses, some of which may now be seen in wine museums, with labourers straining at the huge beams to exert the pressure on the mass of grapes, or else the grapes would be tipped into a small pen and trodden by the naked feet of the vintagers.

The idea of treading the grapes is in fact a very practical one, because it is important, when extracting the juice, not to exert so much pressure that the pips are split and stalks and stems still attached to the bunches of grapes are also crushed: if this happens, the wine will be harsh and bitter. The human foot can break up the grapes without crushing pips or stems. In certain of the great wine regions, notably the port area, treading the grapes was carried on until very recently and a few firms still find this the best method; likewise in the sherry area, for example, where labourers, wearing special boots with rows of nails set in the soles at an angle to catch the pips and pith, once used to tread up and down on the grapes. In case anyone is apprehensive about dirt coming into contact with the wine, it should be stressed that both the feet of the treaders and the boots were scrupulously cleaned beforehand, and in any case the process of fermentation itself is also a means of cleansing the wine; of course, after the wine is made, it is subjected to many subsequent filtering and purifying processes.

Some of the finest wines, including certain great clarets, are still made by teams of skilled workers rubbing the bunches of grapes through huge wooden sieves (the grape juice does not come into contact with anything metallic) but, in general, the grapes are now crushed by different types of mechanical press, the type used depending on the grapes involved and the type of wine to be made.

Making wine
Most grape juice as it runs out of the pressed or crushed grapes is a yellowish-green, rather like grapefruit juice. There are a few grapes which yield pinkish juice, but most grape juice is in no way related in hue to either the red or white wine it ultimately becomes. The colour of all red wines and of some pink or rosé wines is acquired by allowing the skins of the red (or black) grapes to remain with the grape juice (known as must) while it is fermenting. For pink wines, the grape skins are only left in contact with the juice for a very short time, just enough to tint it, but for red wines they may remain in contact with it for some days. When white wines are made,

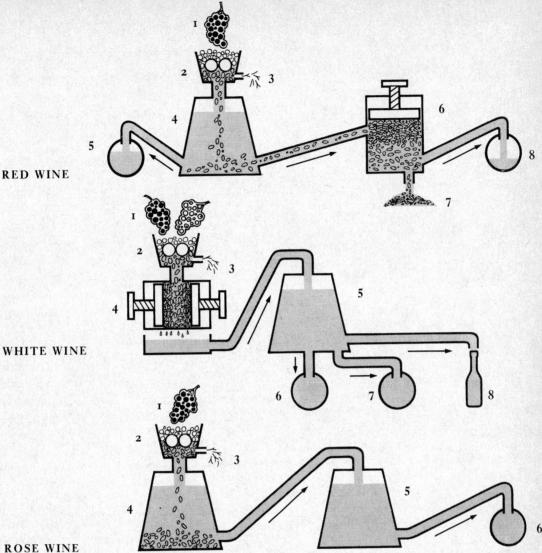

RED WINE

WHITE WINE

ROSE WINE

HOW TABLE WINE IS MADE

RED WINE **1** Red grapes. **2** Crusher. **3** Stalks and pips may be removed here. **4** Fermenting vat: crushed grapes ferment on the skins which impart colour and flavour to red wines. **5** Free-run wine comes without pressing. **6** Press extracts remaining juice from pulp. **7** After pressing, pulp (skins, pips, etc.) can be distilled for cheap brandy (marc). **8** Young red wine.

WHITE WINE **1** Red and white grapes. **2** Crusher and stemmer. **3** Stalks and pips are removed here. **4** Press extracts juice, leaving skins behind which would otherwise colour the juice. **5** Fermenting vat. **6** Sweet wines are drawn off before fermentation is completed and all the sugar is converted into alcohol. **7** Dry wines are left until fermentation is completed. **8** Sparkling wines are drawn off before fermentation is completed, which then continues either in bottle or tank.

ROSÉ WINE **1** Red grapes. **2** Crusher. **3** Stalks and pips may be removed here. **4** First fermenting vat: crushed grapes left with skins until wine has taken on required pink colour; it is then run off, leaving the pulp behind. **5** Second fermenting vat: wine finishes fermenting and is usually dry. **6** Young rosé wine.

the grape skins and all the pips and other matter never come into contact with the juice at all.

When this first stage of wine-making has been accomplished, the wine is probably still in a vat or huge cask or container, together with all the bits and pieces which will inevitably have got in when the grapes were being crushed. The wine is, therefore, run off all this deposit, known as the lees, either into casks, where it will settle down and mature, or into different vats, where it can be prepared for bottling if it is a wine meant for drinking quite soon after the vintage. During the course of its life before bottling it will be clarified (the process is known as fining) and also filtered, and wines that spend a year or more in casks, will be 'racked', which means that they are drawn off from cask to cask leaving behind the deposit which has fallen to the bottom of the cask; this process keeps them in prime condition and enables a check to be made on the contents of each cask.

When the wine is ready to be bottled, which can vary considerably according to the type of wine being made, then the bottles themselves are prepared to receive it. They are cleaned, and for the most delicate wines sterilised and the wine, having been finally inspected, is run into the bottles, stoppered, either with cork or plastic stoppers, which are then 'dressed', which means they are prepared for sale. A capsule is put on over the cork to protect it, the bottle is labelled and the wine is then ready to be sold. All these operations are subject not only to the conditions considered necessary by the individual producers and makers of wine, but are also regulated by legislation, so that such matters as the lettering on the labels, the size and colour of bottles and many other details are all strictly supervised and controlled.

This, in general terms, is how wine is made, and all wines are made in basically the same way. There are, however, different types of wine, and in every vineyard throughout the world there will be slight individual modifications of the basic methods. But the person who drinks for enjoyment – which is the first and most important reason why one should drink wine at all – need not be concerned with these, unless it is found that they add to the interest of wine drinking.

For some people, it is more satisfying to see a demonstration of an elaborate piece of cookery than to eat the finished dish; with others, the enjoyment of the dish is enough. Some people just like to look at a beautiful garden, others are interested in knowing how it was planned and understanding something of the flowers and trees they see. Both can enjoy the experience of the cooking and the garden. So it is with wine: for some people, the more they know about how wine is made, why certain procedures have contributed to certain characteristics, what the vineyard is like, whether the particular year in which the wine was made was hot, cold, wet or dry, the methods followed by the owner of the property and similar details, can all enhance and

Corks
for different
wine bottles are
made from the
bark of the cork-
oak, which grows
in Mediterranean
countries like
Portugal, Spain
and North Africa

deepen the enjoyment of the wine when it is poured into the glass. But for many people the enjoyment is simply that of the wine itself – and there is nothing wrong with this. There is no need whatsoever to know more about how the wine was made than is outlined here; you do not, after all, have to understand how to rear championship cattle in order to enjoy a good steak!

Chapter 2 The Different Types of Wine

To buy confidently your own wine and choose the appropriate bottles for different occasions requires knowledge of the different types of wine – after all, you won't always be in the position of a guest and so enjoy what someone else has chosen for you.

Wine writers and teachers of wine try to do this in various ways, but many of their would-be students find buying and choosing wines difficult to master when there are vast numbers of different foreign names to remember. Besides, over-simplifying wine recommendations can also mean that you spend the rest of your drinking life restricted to perhaps three or four different wines, and possibly live in ignorance of the many other kinds.

Some wine names you ought to try and remember because they relate to the classic wines, which are known throughout the world – even to people with only a slight knowledge of wine – and which, therefore, you should not find difficulty in obtaining anywhere. These classic wines set the standard for other lesser wines, which can then be related to them; however, this doesn't necessarily mean that lesser wines are worse in quality because they happen to be cheaper, or that they are exactly the same because they happen to bear a similar name. It means rather that they possess some kind of general associations, which are helpful. When you learn to cook, you first master the basics before you proceed to something more complicated or venture to create something of your own. When you know in general terms how a basic stew, for example, is made, then you can adapt both ingredients and the method of cooking when copying some version of it, even through the dish in its new guise may bear a complicated foreign name.

Three basic types of wine Exactly the same approach can be adopted with regard to wine. There are thousands, perhaps hundreds of thousands, of wines made throughout the world, but there are only three main types: still wines (which are usually known as table wines), sparkling wines and fortified wines. A small technical point worth bearing in mind is that, since Britain joined the Common Market (the European Economic Community), the E.E.C. now defines fortified wines as liqueur wines; they themselves have not changed and have nothing to do with liqueurs, so the English-speaking drinker will probably find it simplest to continue calling them fortified wines.

Within each of these three categories of wine there is a whole range of tastes from very dry to very sweet, which applies to white, red, and pink or rosé wines. It is very difficult, indeed, to make rigid distinctions between the dryness and sweetness of many wines because these taste sensations obviously depend on personal ideas of what is dry and what is sweet. Although a certain amount of sweetness can be added to some wines (but within certain defined limits), either after they have been made or while they are being made, there may be quite a different understanding of the word 'dry' by one person and its meaning to someone else. Exact controls on this kind of thing are obviously impossible to enforce and in fact some wines bear brand names implying that they are dry, when in fact they are almost medium sweet!

There are also fashions in wines as in everything else, and sometimes there is a vogue for supposedly dry wines, at others for sweeter ones, so without tasting and making up one's own mind, it is difficult to generalize about wines that are in the middle ranges of flavour, as opposed to the extremes of dryness and sweetness.

Table wines As you would suppose, table wines are intended for drinking with food. But, in fact, many of them, particularly the white wines, can be drunk at any time, quite outside the context of meals, and in recent years more and more people have found it most enjoyable to offer a glass of table wine as an apéritif before a meal or as a drink at any time.

Table wines are still wines, that is, they do not sparkle. They include white, both dry and sweet, all the red wines of the world, especially the clarets and red Burgundies, and the popular pink or rosé wines. Various conventions have grown up as regards the suitability of certain kinds of table wine with certain types of food, but these should be taken as suggestions rather than hard and fast rules. Even fashions change in this respect and one can only be definite about certain combinations of some wines with particular dishes which have pleased large numbers of people in the past.

Sparkling wines As the description implies, these are wines that contain bubbles. The majority of sparkling wines and the best known are white, but red and pink sparkling wines are also made. They can be very dry, medium dry, or definitely sweet. The bottles in which they are sold usually have special corks or stoppers held down by some sort of fastener so that they are not blown out of the bottles by the pressure of the gas in the wine. Sparkling wines are sometimes described as all-purpose, and it is true that many of them can be served both with food and at any time.

Fortified wines As the word 'fortified' implies, these wines are made stronger by the addition of spirit, usually brandy, at some stage in their production. Some people have the mistaken idea that, in their various countries of origin, they are unfortified, but this is not so. The truth is that in order to give these wines the ability to withstand the changes of temperature, possible rough handling and general hazards of travel, the alcoholic strength at which they may be shipped is sometimes increased very slightly; however, this change is imperceptible except to the most experienced taster, and is no concern of the person drinking for enjoyment. Mainly because they are higher in alcoholic strength than table or sparkling wines, they are not generally served throughout a meal; however, they can be excellent with certain first courses and last courses, and they are very often served as apéritifs as well as being drunk by themselves between meals. They can vary in style from very dry indeed to lusciously sweet, and they are famous wines for drinking before meals and afterwards.

Vermouth and other wine-based drinks Vermouth is a type of wine slightly higher in alcoholic strength than table wine, and is possibly the oldest form of wine known to man. Essentially, it is aromatised wine, made in the normal way but flavoured or infused with herbs, spices, barks, peels and other additives. Hippocrates, the father of medicine, used aromatised wine both as a preventative and a curative medicine, and his example was followed throughout the ages.

Vermouth has been commercially produced since the end of the 18th century, and originally it was intended to be drunk straight, rather than be mixed with spirits, as happened when cocktails became fashionable in the early 1900's. Now the wheel has turned full circle and vermouth is once again becoming popular as a straight drink.

Many other apéritif drinks are based on wine, like Dubonnet and St. Raphael, as well as those so popular in many European countries. There are quite a number of other wines as well which are naturally high in alcoholic strength without being fortified, which are sometimes offered as drinks between-times.

An enormous amount has been written about every single one of the principal wines of the world, but here they will be described in general terms only, so that you will know what they are like, how to select them, and when and how to serve them. Anyone who wants to study them in more detail should consult the Bibliography.

What the drinks should do

Apéritifs   The word apéritif comes from a Latin verb which means 'to open', and this is exactly what this type of drink should do – open the gastronomic door to whatever party is going on and, either by providing a refreshment or stimulant, prepare the palate and, consequently, the digestive juices. The occasions on which apéritifs are offered can vary widely, so they themselves can come from an enormous range of drinks: dry white table wines, sparkling wines, fortified wines like sherry, white port and sercial Madeira, spirits, either straight or with simple additions, and complicated cocktails. It is up to the host in every instance to decide the kind of apéritif that is going to be most enjoyable and appropriate for the kind of hospitality that is to follow.

Many people think that it is necessary to offer a large choice of apéritif drinks, whether you are having a stand-up drinks party or offering a drink before a meal but, in fact, the trend nowadays is entirely towards simplicity and, unless you have staff (either your own or hired for the occasion) or family and friends to help you in serving, it is best to restrict the choice to one or two drinks. Usually people are quite content to be offered a single drink with a non-alcoholic alternative available.

If you are inviting people to a meal, then the apéritif drinks should form part of the drinks programme as a whole (see Chapter 6). If you are having people round just for drinks, then the circumstances may well determine what is to be served: for example, people do not usually want very strong spirit-based drinks in the middle of the day if they are going to have to go back to work, at least not in quantity; but a drink with a slight kick to it can be a great pick-you-up at the end of the day.

To avoid possible unpleasant after-effects, it's best not to mix the grape and the grain if you are going to serve very fine wines, when the only spirit which is really suitable beforehand is a grape brandy of some sort; ideally however, you should have a glass of sherry, dry vermouth, or a dry sparkling wine, preferably Champagne, before a meal accompanied by wines of top quality, instead of spirits which dull the taste buds. Remember that a sparkling wine gives a good lift and creates a party spirit quickly because of the carbon dioxide retained in the wine, whereas a table wine is a lighter drink. A fortified wine, such as sherry, being stronger in alcohol than a table wine, provides the necessary lift and because it is a wine, it will not stun or alter the palate before the wines to follow.

The thing to do, when deciding which apéritifs to offer, is to make up your mind as to what the apéritif should do: should it give people a quick lift, be pleasant enough to drink for some time (such as a light table wine which you may choose to serve at a drinks party or buffet), or not only give them a slight lift but also sharpen their appetites? It is up to you to decide, and the following sections on the main wines will guide you in making your choice.

But one generalization about apéritifs is really important: they should refresh and stimulate, never stun or cloy the palate. This is why, ideally, they should always be served cool or cold. This does not mean to say that they they must be iced, but everyone knows that a cool drink is more refreshing than a tepid one. It may surprise some people to learn that sherry should be served chilled, especially when it is offered as an apéritif, because this brings out its beautiful flavour and smell. The wine is simply more enjoyable served like this.

There is a popular belief that it is 'better' always to choose a dry drink as an apéritif, but a number of drinks which are consumed in enormous quantities in the belief that they are 'dry' are, in fact, nothing of the kind! For example, certain very well-known brands of sherry follow the marketing maxim of one of the greatest of sherry producers, 'Call it dry but make it sweet', at least as far as export requirements are concerned. Many people enjoy a sweet drink and, for someone who is tired, a little sweetness in their drink may be extremely acceptable and exactly the right fillip. So the snobbery about 'drinking dry' is quite unjustified.

At the same time, people do have difficulty in taking more than a very small quantity of an extremely sweet drink if they are going on to eat a meal. A young person might be able to dispose of chocolates or sweets and then sit down to a good meal, but as we grow up this simply isn't possible because sweetness cuts the appetite. Exactly the same thing happens to wine if a very sweet wine or mixed drink is drunk immediately before food: any really dry wine served immediately afterwards will taste acid, and whether the wine is high or low in alcohol, very few people will want to take more than a little of anything extremely sweet. This is the only reason why the very sweet wines tend to be served at the end of a meal instead of at the beginning; however, if you have an hour or so to spare before eating, and you are not going to serve a bone-dry wine immediately after your sweet apéritif, then there is no reason why you should not then enjoy this kind of drink.

One final point, many people who find that a drink before a meal helps their enjoyment of the food and digestion, but who do not always drink wine with a meal, do enjoy medium-sweet drinks beforehand.

To recap, here are suitable apéritifs:

> Champagne or a quality sparkling wine, of dry or dryish character.
> Dry vermouth (e.g. white vermouth, mixed vermouth, or vermouth cassis).
> Fortified wines: fino or amontillado sherry, sercial Madeira, or white port.

Table wines: nothing too assertive; virtually anything made from the
Riesling grape, and other dryish white wines, of light to medium
character. Unless the apéritif table wine is to be drunk with the
first course as well, you should make sure your choice of wine with
the first course is either of the same style as the apéritif table wine,
or at least not dryer or of lesser quality.

Spirit-based drinks: choose brandy-based ones before a meal at which
very fine wines are to be served; otherwise, choose simpler mixtures,
according to taste, before meals at which medium or everyday quality
wines are to be served.

Non-alcoholic drinks should also be available.

Table wines   It is important to realize that wine, like any other beverage (except plain
water) is a food as well as a drink; it should, therefore, be an integral part of
the menu. Food that is absolutely dry is difficult to eat and digest. If you have
nothing to lubricate it, in the form of some sort of fat, nor to soften it,
in the form of a liquid, the food will be uncomfortable not only in your
mouth but also after swallowing. The digestive juices, which act upon food
so as to process it and make it into acceptable fuel for the body, find it difficult
to do their job if they do not themselves receive some stimulation; in too
concentrated a form they can become just as ineffectual as when they are too
diluted.

Just as the food must not be of such a nature as to make the wine taste
peculiar or not taste at all, so the wine also must not overwhelm the food
or alter its taste. Ideally, the wine should make the food taste better, while
the food should set off the wine. If, for a moment, you can think of the wine
really as an adjunct to the food, rather like an extra sauce, you will then
appreciate how it should fit into the meal.

Another point to bear in mind when choosing a wine for a meal is that
unlike food its quality remains fairly constant. As a meal progresses the
food may get cold, the choicest portions are usually served first, and the
overall appearance of the dish becomes less attractive, whereas the wine may
improve and, as far as some of the finer wines are concerned, their progressive
aeration during the course of the meal will make them seem much more
pleasant. The palate can be greatly altered by the food, so that many wines,
which at the outset of a meal might not have impressed the drinkers very
much, can become increasingly delicious through the various courses.

It may be said with fair accuracy that wines served with food should play
the part of one of the partners in a successful marriage – without it ever
being obvious which is dominant! So it is always worthwhile giving equal
consideration to the table wines and the menu. If you simply decide to buy a
wine to go with a meal half an hour or so beforehand, you are being as casual

as if you decide what to eat for dinner on the spur of the moment. Of course, last-minute catering is something inevitable, but then the reserve store cupboard – for drinks as well as foodstuffs – plays its part.

Always think of the table wine as being as important as the meal, and try to achieve a balance between the two. Let the wine play its part – as a digestive, a complement to the food, saver of the situation if something goes wrong in the kitchen, a talking-point as much as any dish, and something that the host and hostess can enjoy without too much trouble, even if the stresses of getting a meal, either en famille or when entertaining company, are inclined to make them feel that they would be just as happy with a poached egg! And even if you think that your family and guests are not really 'up to' appreciating a good or fine wine, never hesitate to offer it – for your own sake – whenever possible. If everything else goes wrong and the company are at their worst, you at least can enjoy a good drink so that your digestion, your endurance and your temper remain unimpaired.

Fortified wines   As many of the best-known fortified wines, such as the dryer sherries, white port, sercial Madeira, are also the best-known apéritif wines, this section might almost be devoted to the fortified wines intended either for between-time or after-meal consumption. But the fortified wines do, in general, have a specific role.

By virtue of their higher alcoholic strength the fortified wines provide, discreetly, additional 'lift' and nourishment. Before a meal, they make their effect felt just slightly more swiftly than a table wine, without the real 'kick' of a spirit-based drink. So anyone feeling nervous, tired or simply very hungry can get extra stimulation and nourishment from a fortified wine. After a meal, the same applies: a meal can be tiring, albeit agreeably so; the digestion may require help, the social circumstances, when people settle down to talk, may require stimulation but without getting everyone excited, and also to give a little sensuous pleasure. The fine fortified wines should never be drunk in haste. They are for sipping and savouring with, perhaps, some talk about them. They are gentle yet complex drinks, offering immense pleasure and interest to everyone.

How strong is   People tend to have rather comic ideas about 'strong drink'. And just as no
your drink?   one should drink wine to quench their thirst (water is the best quencher of all), so no one should approach wine as something that is going to make them drunk, any more than they would approach a good meal with the notion that it was going to make them sick. To indulge in either to excess is courting disaster, but in moderation they can be pure enjoyment.

Alcohol is as necessary to wine as the skeleton is to the human body: it is the framework, the very heart of wine. But there is much more to wine than alcohol, so the wine drinker should pay no more attention to alcoholic content than to what makes an enjoyable drink. Good wine, in all price ranges, should be made so that the alcoholic content is there without being noticeable, otherwise it unbalances the wine. Sometimes people talk about a wine being 'heavy' or 'heady' when what they really mean is that it is either very fragrant or overwhelmingly assertive in flavour, or simply makes demands on their interest or intelligence – but it can still be quite light in alcohol. Indeed, there are some wines which the French describe as 'traitors' simply because they go down very easily and yet pack an unexpected punch so that the drinker feels quite sleepy afterwards. It is impossible to judge the exact amount of alcohol in a wine just by tasting; this is a job for the laboratory and is best left to the wine technician.

Few of us realize that even stone ginger beer contains a small proportion of alcohol. But even less widely known is that the strengths of wines and spirits are partly regulated by the Customs and Excise authorities, because the duty on wines and spirits is assessed according to their alcoholic strength. There is, therefore, no likelihood of the drinker getting a high strength wine, such as a fortified wine, instead of a table wine.

Anyone interested in knowing the approximate strengths of the different types of drink should consult the table opposite. Variations can occur within each category, but you may be sure that it would be unsatisfactory for a particular wine to go lower than the category limits, and uneconomic as well if it went above them.

The way in which alcoholic strength is stated on wine labels is in terms of percentage of alcohol by volume, a system also known as Gay Lussac after the man who evolved it in the first place. The system of proof or Sikes is rather more complicated and, now that Britain is a member of the Common Market, it is likely that the Gay Lussac system will be the one you are most likely to come across. If you buy a bottle of wine in a French supermarket, for example, you will see the alcoholic strength marked on the label: 12°, 11·5° and so on. Some people rather mistakenly suppose that a wine slightly higher in alcohol in the table wine range will be better than one that is lower, but this is by no means so. What is true is that the wine of a slightly higher strength will probably travel better and, simply because of this additional strength, it may cost a little more. The actual strength does not relate directly to your enjoyment of the wine. It would seem appropriate at this point to have a look at the problem of hangovers.

The hangover problem   People vary and so do drinks, and although it is easy to say that the best way to deal with a hangover is to avoid getting one, there are nevertheless times when they seem to materialize out of nowhere!

Apart from strictly limiting how much you drink, there are several ways

TYPES OF WINES AND SPIRITS	ALCOHOLIC CONTENT (*Percentage of alcohol by volume – Gay Lussac*)
Table wines Red, white and rosé **Sparkling wines** Also slightly sparkling wines known as pétillant or spritzig, in particular the 'Green Wines' of Portugal	7°–14°
Fortified wines Sherry, Port, Madeira, Marsala, and other fortified wines	18°–21°
Vermouth and other wine-based apéritifs Dubonnet, St. Raphael, etc.	16°–20°
Brandy Different kinds vary in alcoholic strength and also in the particular properties they possess, which can in turn affect the result they have on the drinker almost as much as the actual alcoholic content. This is why you risk a worse hangover with certain spirits and not others, even though they may be of similar strength!	45°–55°
Liqueurs & fruit cordials	30°–60°

to avoid the unpleasant effects of alcohol. The best are to have something to eat while drinking, and to dilute any spirits with something non-alcoholic.

If you drink plenty of water or mineral water when you think you may have to drink more wine than you are really used to, this also has the same preventative advantage. To drink without eating is always to risk drinking more than one realizes; it is not for nothing that the traditional Spanish accompaniment to sherry is known as *tapas* (little savoury appetizers), a word which means 'covers', signifying something to cover or blot up the alcohol.

It is not quite true that mixing 'grape with grain' (in other words combining drinks based on spirits with wines) is always responsible for a hangover. But it is true that a hangover is the result of the stomach being upset, which it certainly will be if it has to cope with too great a mixture of drinks. It is also wise to stop drinking *before* you think you have had enough, as unless you are used to a fairly regular intake of alcohol, it is very difficult to be sure when you have reached this stage, and by then it may be too late.

And never, in any circumstances, do more than toy with a mixed drink when you are not absolutely sure of its contents. Some people think it amusing to concoct drinks which taste comparatively harmless but are very strong; at best this is silly, at worst extremely dangerous, and it is sound sense either to tip such a drink away or refuse it altogether. If, for some reason, you are simply given an unknown mixture and can't get rid of it, then take as little as possible and, when you can, plenty of water.

Having 'one for the road' has already been universally condemned as dangerous, whether you are driving or simply walking home. It is equally unwise to get into a car or even accompany on foot anyone who has disregarded this advice. Apart from dulling the senses, because you have already exceeded how much you can cope with, alcohol reduces body heat so that you can get a chill. If you really want a final drink, the time to have it is when you get indoors and can keep warm.

Should you, when you return from a party for example, realize that you have had too much to drink, then take as much water as you can drink, plus some fizzy health salts and aspirin before you go to bed, and repeat the dose as soon as you wake up in the morning. You should take as much liquid as you can with the aspirin anyway, and you can substitute cold milk for water, if you like, but certainly not any sort of fruit juice, which will merely irritate your over-acid stomach further.

That morning-after feeling – nausea, headache, great thirst and generally out of sorts – is best dealt with by taking the aspirin and health salts as before, plus a warm bath and a cold shower, as well as eating some breakfast. You probably won't feel up to any of these remedies, but you need liquid to dilute any alcohol still in your system, and something to calm the stomach and give you energy while you are recovering. A brisk walk will probably complete the cure, but if you still feel miserable, then try any of the recognized remedies, like a measure of Fernet Branca, Underberg Bitters, Ferro China, Elixir, either with water or soda, if you wish. About a teaspoonful of Angostura Bitters in a large glass of tonic water can be equally effective. But don't, otherwise, indulge in the 'hair of the dog', or anything else alcoholic until you feel completely better.

One small crumb of comfort is that very few people have not, at one time or another in their lives, endured considerable morning-after malaise through no really violent excesses on their part; certain drinks do seem to affect some people almost savagely, while at other times you may be very tired, and on such occasions it takes very little to upset the stomach. 'Alcoholic remorse', one sign of a genuine hangover, is, alas, likely to be present on such occasions, but the sufferer should not automatically assume that his or her behaviour was absolutely inexcusable on the previous evening – being the life and soul of the party is by no means the same thing as having been disagreeably drunk; however, if you are nursing a hangover you probably won't see the difference. Try to tell yourself – in between glasses of water – that your friends probably noticed nothing at all.

Last but not least, if you have to minister to anyone who, again through no fault of their own, has had too much to drink, give them plenty of water or soda water, keep them warm and, if they are really unwell, be prepared for them to be sick; if they are, they will recover quicker, even though they may feel they are going from bad to worse. And never, in any circumstances, persuade anyone to take a drink or another drink against their will or if you yourself feel that they have already had enough. Some people regard this as 'fun' but it is totally irresponsible and can be downright dangerous not only for the person concerned but for other people as well.

Chapter 3 *The Principal Wines of the World*

The classic table wines

It is as difficult to generalize about table wines and what they are like as it is about human beings, but as a beginning has to be made somewhere, let's start by singling out the world-famous table wines whose characteristics can be detected in other, lesser-known wines. If you know about these classics, then, when you are shopping, you can ask anyone who seems reasonably well-informed for a wine 'like' a particular well-known name.

Of course, as you get to know wines in more detail, this is rather like saying that someone with blue eyes, fair hair and a straight nose is like someone else with blue eyes, fair hair and a straight nose; they may not really be alike at all, as you get to know them, but the superficial similarities are a point of contact. After all, a stew is a stew, whether it is steak and kidney, jugged hare or coq au vin but, if you feel like cooking or eating 'a stew' you may enjoy any one of these.

So here are general descriptions of the well-known wines of the world and the kind of dishes which they usually partner satisfactorily to the enjoyment of many people. You can be helped by tradition and convention and as you come to know more about wine, you will probably begin to disagree with some of the descriptions given here; this is all to the good for it shows that you are making up your own mind, and are sorting out wines just as one sorts out people. The more you know about wines, the more different they will seem, but each one will fall into a general descriptive category such as are given here.

France

Sometimes people feel that writers on wine devote too much space to French wines. The reason is that France produces an enormous quantity of both fine and everyday wines – red, white, still, sparkling and pink in all its

Ammerschwihr in Alsace is one of many quaint villages on the Wine Road

tones – and for centuries now the fame of the finer wines of France has spread throughout the world and has established certain standards as to how fine wines in various categories should taste. The grapes from which some of these wines are made, either making use of a single grape variety or a mixture, are also world famous, so that if you know a little about a French wine made from a particular grape, you may well be able to pick up some family likeness with a wine made from the same grape but produced many thousands of miles away.

ALSACE   This beautiful region, in the north-east of France, produces a range of white wines which are still comparatively reasonable in price. They must not in any way be taken as poor relations of German wines because, even though some of the grapes from which they are made are the same as those used in many German vineyards, the different climate and soil of Alsace gives their wines individuality and they deserve appraisal entirely in their own right.

Many non-vintage wines are made, but the finer wines will have a vintage date on their labels; Alsatian wines, however, tend to be at their best when drunk young and fresh. There are a few site names used, referring to specific vineyards, but within these vineyards several types of wine may be made. In general, however, the wines are called after the grapes from which they are made, although it is important to realize that every shipper will stress the individuality and distinction of his particular wines; sometimes a shipper will also add a qualification to the ordinary name of the wine, indicating that the wine is of a specially high standard, such as the words 'réserve exceptionelle'.

What the wines are like The **Riesling** grape (pronounced so that the first syllable rhymes with 'geese'), which makes some of the world's noblest wines, here produces very fragrant wines, fruity and dry, and those of great years can be extremely full-bodied. They make excellent apéritif or between-times drinks, and can partner many fish dishes, notably trout and fresh-water fish; the more expensive quality wines are even capable of accompanying not too strongly-flavoured meat dishes, such as boiled chicken, chicken poached in wine, plain roast poultry or veal, and sweetbreads done in wine.

The **Gewürztraminer** grape (put the accent on the second syllable and approximate pronunciation to Gerverststramna) makes particularly spicy wines, they are very popular and, like the Rieslings, can be drunk as apéritifs or between-times, as well as with food. They are good wines to choose if you are eating something rather rich, such as a meat pâté, although they can also be excellent with a fish dish which has a fairly rich sauce, or they can partner fat fish, such as salmon. These are the wines to start your study of Alsace.

Muscat wines have particularly scented bouquets – they really do smell of the grape, unlike many – and are fairly full-bodied. They are soft and 'bloomy' in character, although dry, and are of such a definite fragrance and flavour that you either like them very much or not at all. They can be drunk as apéritifs, or with fish or lightly-flavoured meat dishes, when a particularly fragrant wine is required.

Sylvaner wines are light and fresh; they are eminently suitable as apéritifs or for drinking at any time, or perhaps with a first course when something crisp and fairly light is required.

Pinot grapes make dry, fairly full-bodied wines, which are suitable for accompanying meat or fish; because they have a certain forcefulness as well, they can partner dishes such as pork, when a very straightforward dry white wine, without much subtlety but with plenty of body, is required.

BORDEAUX This region in the south-west of France produces the highest proportion of fine wines, both red and white, in the whole of France. The red wines are known in Britain as claret, and there are many links between the United Kingdom and Bordeaux, because for over 300 years, this area belonged to the English crown until the time of Joan of Arc. The variety of wines made here is enormous: lovers of claret would say that there was a claret to go with anything and to be served on any occasion when a red wine is required, while the wines range between light and dry to the greatest sweet wines of France.

The important red wine grapes are the Cabernet sauvignon, Cabernet franc, and the Merlot range, while the important white wine grapes are the Sauvignon blanc, Sémillon, and Muscadelle.

Red wines

What are they like Although the greatest red Bordeaux can live for a very long time – even longer than a human being – it must never be assumed that age is in itself an asset; some of the 'little' or less superior red Bordeaux are definitely at their best when they are comparatively young, and an enormous quantity of non-vintage wine is made as well. With the greatest red wines, it is the individuality of the estate (Château is the most usual designation of this) that makes the wine, plus the particular characteristics of a vintage year which will be marked, so that it is both important to obtain advice when you are buying an expensive wine in this category, and also to try and remember what you thought of it when you tried it.

The Médoc which sticks out like a great tongue of land northwards from Bordeaux, is where some of the finest red wines come from. The main communes or parishes within this district are noted for different characteristics:

St Estèphe: These wines tend to mature more slowly than many others from the Médoc. At the outset they possess a hard, almost stalky flavour rather like raw rhubarb, which some people find unattractive, but which can be indicative of a fine future. They are interesting, classic clarets, but if you are a beginner you may find them less attractive than others, though you are sure to come to share the claret-lovers' enthusiasm for them as you gain knowledge of this great wine.

Pauillac: This commune includes three great first growths (*see Glossary*), and many people would say that the great Pauillacs are the greatest red wines in the world. They, too, can possess a slight hardness when they are very young, but they are usually firm, almost masculine wines, with a most beautiful bouquet (it reminds some people of the inside of cigar boxes) and a long, lingering flavour and aftertaste. These are wines for important occasions, and, if you choose cleverly, you can please almost anyone with a great Pauillac – including the person who thinks he prefers Burgundy to claret!

St. Julien: 'Velvety' is an adjective often applied to the fine wines of St. Julien, which are extremely fragrant and have what might be described as a beautiful texture; they are also very elegant and charming. A St. Julien might be a very good starting point for knowledge of fine claret; the wines are not too demanding if you want to serve them in the middle of the day, or as the first of several clarets at an important dinner.

Margaux: Fruit, great fragrance and charm characterize the Margaux wines at their best. They tend to be more assertive than St. Julien wines, but have a very elegant style and, again, are easy to like immediately.

These then are the main districts of the Médoc; there are many others, some of them making wines to the standârd of classed growths (*see Glossary*), which are also very fine. The classed growths tend to take longer to mature than the bourgeois growths (*see Glossary*), but from the wines of the Médoc in general it is always possible to find a red wine suitable for any type of meal requiring a red wine. The very finest Médocs are possibly best reserved for great joints, game and anything roast, which is served rather simply; with wines of this calibre, the wise hostess will let the wines shine and the food remain a simple but perfect accompaniment.

Graves: It sometimes surprises people to know that very fine red wines are made in the Graves district of Bordeaux, which is more readily associated with white wines, and indeed there are also some very great ones. In general, the red wines have a particular subtlety, a bouquet which reminds some people of flowers, or which evokes the description 'spicy' in others, and they can have a very gentle, lingering flavour with special charm.

These, too, are the wines for straightforward, simple roasts and grills, in fact any food requiring a very fine red wine.

St. Emilion: Some of the famous St. Emilions have been called the Burgundies of Bordeaux, and they can be very big or large-scale, fruity wines, possessing immediate appeal and a full-bodied character. These are definitely wines for the beginner to enjoy, because their taste is easy to appreciate and, as well as going with roasts and grills, they can accompany meat dishes with wine sauces and even the more luxurious type of casserole or pie.

Pomerol: In the past, the wines of Pomerol tended to be lumped together with those of St. Emilion; in fact they are quite different, the soil accounting for a certain lightness and elegance, which is found in the wines of the finer estates. They are usually fairly full-bodied, but possess a light, almost fresh, character, and they can be served with all red meat and roasts, the smaller-scale wines being comparatively undemanding, while the greater ones are on a par with all but the very finest wines of the Médoc.

Other red Bordeaux Red wines are made in many other districts of Bordeaux, including **Fronsac, Bourg, Blaye**, and the **Premières Côtes**. As yet, they all tend to be 'little' wines, a reflection on their character, rather than on their quality, for these relatively unknown wines can offer great value for money and can appeal very much to people who want clarets which are easy to drink, yet neither make too many demands on them nor overwhelm the food. A word of warning to the inexperienced: several properties have names which are similar to or even exactly like those of some of the more famous estates. There is nothing suspicious about this, because if an estate has enjoyed a particular name for several hundred years, there is no reason why it should suddenly change it, any more than someone who has the same name as someone else should do so. But just make sure you study the label carefully before you complain to a wine waiter or wine merchant about the bottle of claret not being 'what it ought to be', as this will clearly state the district from which the wine comes, making it easy to identify correctly.

Commune wines Wines from the communes or parishes, such as St. Julien, Margaux, and St. Emilion, which do not bear a vintage date are ready for drinking as soon as you buy them. They do not require any special care, apart from that necessary to the service of any good wine, so this makes them very good, everyday wines.

It should be realized that some of the red wines produced in the Bordeaux region were formerly made by peasant proprietors who, however carefully they made the wines of their own small property, could never expect them to compete with those of the great estates; such wines would not necessarily benefit by long-term ageing. In recent years, therefore, there has been a move to make such wines by subjecting them to a process whereby they remain typical claret, but are ready to drink in a comparatively short space of time, without the hardness and generally unattractive style which usually make some people think that they do not like fine claret if they drink it too young. There is nothing wrong at all in using such very small wines in this way, because they supplement the choice of wines for good everyday drinking, which everyone requires, without impinging on the greater pleasures which can be obtained by occasional indulgence in the finer wines of the area.

White wines

Many districts in the Bordeaux region produce white wine, but the principal ones are **Graves, Entre-Deux-Mers, Blaye, Bourg, Graves de Vayres**, and the **Premières Côtes de Bordeaux** (this is mainly a red wine region within Entre-Deux-Mers, but good white wines are also made). Very few white wines are made in the Médoc.

What the wines are like These white wines vary from very light and dry, to those of a rounded, rather supple, style, which can be medium sweet. Some people are unnecessarily affected about 'insipid white Bordeaux' but, while it is true that the dry white wines of this region will never be as large in scale as some of the great wines of other French regions, nor as palate-scrapingly dry as, say, a Muscadet or

Chablis, they can be fine, delicate, and lightly fruity, can appeal to many drinkers and are also useful for serving as apéritifs as well as with fish. In their home region, of course, they accompany many of the shellfish dishes, and they are pleasant drinking with lightly-flavoured food, both meat and fish.

Sweet white wines The greatest sweet wines of France come from the district of **Sauternes**, south of the city of Bordeaux and embracing the smaller **Barsac** area. The sweet wines are made by allowing the grapes to remain on the vines long enough to be affected by the action of a natural fungus, called 'la pourriture noble' or noble rot; this shrivels up the skins and acts upon the juice inside each grape, so that only a single luscious drop is left. The fully-ripe grapes have to be picked one by one as the rot develops and only in exceptional years can they be picked bunch by bunch. Until about a century ago, the wines of this area were dry, or at least dryish, and the story has it that the steward at Château Yquem was ordered to wait to make his vintage until the return of his master; this was delayed by illness and in desperation, the shrivelled grapes, upon which the noble rot had meanwhile been acting, were thrown into the press. To everyone's astonishment, a magnificent sweet wine was made. (*See illustration overleaf.*)

What the wines are like The great Sauternes and Barsac wines are golden, luscious, and have a distinct flowery bouquet. It is true that they are such great wines, and with such a concentrated fruity flavour, that you do not want to drink more than a small amount at a time; but despite their sweetness they are not, or should not be, in the least cloying. There is a slight difference between the Sauternes and the Barsacs: the Sauternes begin sweet, continue sweet and end sweet, whereas the Barsacs have a curious dry finish, and a freshness noticeable after swallowing when one breathes out. Some of the great properties here are now producing a dry white wine as well, and this too has a marked flowery fragrance and fruity flavour.

The wines from the vineyards of **Cérons**, between the Graves and Sauternes, possess something of the dryness of a good white Graves and a small scale version of Sauterne's sweetness; across the river Garonne, the wines of **Sainte-Croix-du-Mont** slightly resemble small-scale Barsacs, and those of **Loupiac** are a little like mini-Sauternes.

The great Sauternes have recently fallen rather out of fashion, because of the mistaken belief that it is better to drink dry wines, but if this prejudice can be overcome and if the wines are served correctly, then they are wonderful and very enjoyable. And because they have suffered from the vagaries of fashion in drinking they are, at least at the present time, still bargains as regards price.

Sweet wines, particularly the great ones, should be chilled to a lower temperature than the dry wines, and are wonderful drinks to finish a good meal; but usually a single glass is enough because of the intensity of the flavour. On their home ground, they are sometimes served with foie gras, but this is a very specialized taste indeed, and it is perhaps as well to experiment before trying out this costly combination on a dinner party. Serve these magnificent wines with fine dessert fruit, or a rather simple fruity pudding; they are too luscious for anything very sweet or excessively creamy.

This is the kind of wine that can also be very pleasant served between-times, or perhaps if people come in during an evening after dinner. The smaller scale sweetish wines are for drinking virtually any time and, of course, can also be served at the end of the meal. As an opened bottle can be kept for about two days in a refrigerator you can enjoy a single glass without a feeling of extravagance.

BEAUJOLAIS Sometimes wine lists put the wines of Beaujolais in with those of Burgundy, but the two are quite different even though the regions touch and, therefore, it seems sensible to consider them separately.

What the wine is like Beaujolais is a word that has earned an ill reputation in recent years, but this is partly because too many people expect it to be something which true good Beaujolais never has been – it should be an easy-going fruity wine, not too profound in flavour, and have a 'more-ish' quality that makes you want to drink it in gulps rather than sips; only the Gamay grape produces wines like this. Not for nothing is the motto of the Beaujolais wine fraternity, 'Empty the casks!'.

Although a little white Beaujolais is made, by far the greater part of the production is red, and a beautiful bright red at that. There are several grades of Beaujolais: **Beaujolais, Beaujolais Supérieure, Beaujolais-Villages**, or for the finer examples, the wines of the individual parishes or villages of **Brouilly, Côte de Brouilly, Chénas, Chiroubles, Fleurie, Juliénas, Morgon, Moulin-à-Vent**, and **Saint Amour**. Each one of these finer wines is different: the first two tend to be rather profound and large-scale, while Chiroubles and Saint Amour are extremely fruity; Fleurie has a particularly attractive fragrance, Juliénas tends to be more meaty in texture, Morgon is rather hard until it matures, and Moulin-à-Vent has a stony flavour, which can be extremely attractive when the wine has developed a little. A very few individual vineyard names may sometimes be found on the labels of the finer wines.

Beaujolais is traditionally at its most enjoyable when it is fairly young, but it should be stressed that this varies according to year – from some vintages

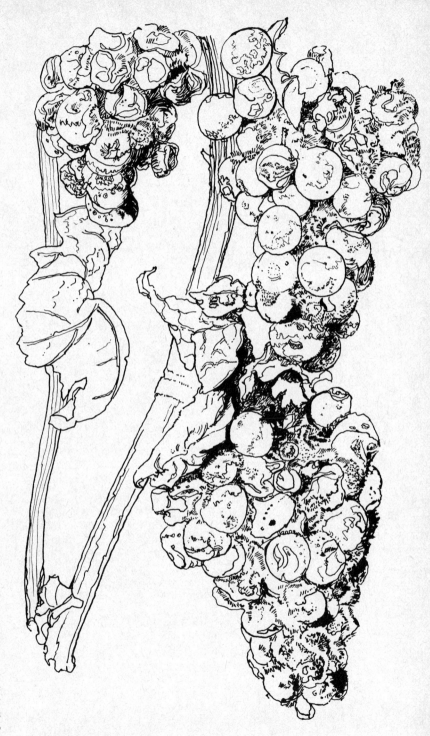

Grapes affected by
noble rot, a natural
fungus which
shrivels up the
fruit and concen-
trates the juice
to a single sweet
and luscious
drop

the wine can go on maturing for eight years or even more; with others, it is at its best between two and five years old.

In recent years there has been a great vogue for drinking the very young wine, a fashion started by the restaurateurs of Dijon, and subsequently Paris, who offered Beaujolais straight from the cask when it was only about a month old, immediately after its first fermentation. As with many fashions, this one has been rather abused; now certain Beaujolais are deliberately 'hit on the head' by an adjusted control of the fermentation, so that they are virtually 'finished' wines when no more than five or six weeks old, and, sadly, never have a chance of growing up to show their more adult charm and appeal.

To drink some of the 'young' Beaujolais made in this way when they are over a year old is to risk a less enjoyable experience than drinking Beaujolais ought always to be. There are different types of this young wine, with phrases like *Vin de l'Année, Nouveau,* and *Primeur* appearing on labels, each one having a slightly different significance. By all means try this type of Beaujolais and see what it is like, but it is generally fair to say that, whichever one you try, the wine will probably be less enjoyable by the March of the year following its vintage, which is when, ideally, the second fermentation should be finishing in a normal wine, and after which ordinary Beaujolais can grow up gracefully and be enjoyable by the time it is a year old. A 'young' Beaujolais, that is one that has been specially treated for rapid sale and consumption, is unlikely to develop well after the first six months of its life.

White Beaujolais is also beginning to enjoy immense popularity. It is a dry, moderately full-bodied wine, without much subtlety, and is a multi-purpose wine, for apéritif drinking or serving with foods requiring a fairly robust, unsubtle wine as a partner.

A wine called **Saint Véran**, which is sometimes described as white Beaujolais, is similar in style but is actually a type of Mâcon, and in fact comes from an area enjoying a newly-created *appellation contrôlée* (*see page* 108).

BURGUNDY   This is a region within which some of the greatest white and red wines of France are produced, yet it is much smaller in area than the Bordeaux region, and, in the past, before strict controls were instituted and enforced, a great deal of 'Burgundy' was made to appeal to the taste of people who liked a certain type of wine, but which rarely bore any relation to genuine Burgundy at all. There have been many instances of self-styled 'experts' rejecting the genuine article in favour of some distorted version of Burgundy, aimed entirely at a market whose taste had already been deformed by certain commercialized wines. At the same time, it is only fair to say that the public has a right to what it wants, and the only thing to be deplored is that, in so many instances, what it wants as far as both red and white wines are con-

A statue erected
to the renowned
winemakers of
Beaujolais

cerned, can bear little resemblance at all to the traditional style of fine white and red Burgundy.

White wines

The **Chablis** district lying somewhat apart from the main Burgundy region, produces a very specialized white Burgundy from Chardonnay grapes: it is very light in colour, with a greenish glint, which much so-called 'Chablis' never possesses, and is very dry indeed, really much too dry for the taste of many people who are beginning their appreciation of wine. There are different grades of Chablis, ranging from **Petit Chablis** and **Chablis** to the wines bearing the names of the individual vineyards of the various sites or great growths.

What the wines are like

Some Chablis can be wines of a very large-scale character indeed, capable of partnering rich, fine fish dishes, but all are bone-dry. In fact many people who know Chablis truly would agree that it is neither a wine for every fish nor for everyday drinking. True Chablis can never be cheap because the vineyards are virtually allotment size, and the wine is produced in really small quantities, nor can genuine Chablis ever be sold by the glass or en carafe. You may get a perfectly good white wine when ordering something of this kind, but it simply *cannot*, for economic reasons, be Chablis.

Around the town of Beaune are some of the finest of the **Côte de Beaune** vineyards producing the white wines of Burgundy, **Meursault** and **Puligny** being particularly notable. These wines (also made from Chardonnay grapes) vary from light to medium gold in colour, and they too can be very big in style, with a wonderful freshness and subtle bouquet, as well as an infinitely shaded flavour.

Great white Burgundies can be the most all-purpose wines in the world, because they are possibly the only white wines which can achieve sufficient grandeur of character to partner even rich meat dishes as well as fish. They are all dry, they can live for a surprisingly long time, and the finer examples can never be cheap. A fine Burgundy is always a great wine, and it is important, when you choose it to accompany the first course, to make sure that you have something worthy coming afterwards, or else the first wine of the meal will be the star of the evening!

Good white wines are also made around **Chalon** and **Mâcon**, and today, with prices of the finer wines soaring, it is these that can give both great pleasure, thanks to modern developments in vinification, and be virtually all-purpose drinking on any occasion when a white wine is required, both with food and outside the context of meals.

Red wines

The greatest red Burgundies come from the region known as the **Côte d'Or** (Golden Slope), which runs from just south of the town of Dijon to the town of Beaune. The Côte d'Or consists of two districts: the **Côte de Nuits,** from just south of Dijon to Nuits-Saint-Georges, whose wines tend to be the very finest examples, sensitive and with many shades of fragrance and flavour, and the **Côte de Beaune**, around Beaune, whose wines tend to be firmer and more straightforward, although possessing appeal and nobility.

What the wines are like The wines, which are made from the great Pinot noir grape, are velvety in style and should be delicate rather than assertive and 'soupy'. Much depends, of course, on the vintage and on the particular wine, but people who have the idea that Burgundy is a big, rich, overwhelming wine have never tasted a really fine, genuine red wine from this region. There should never be any obvious fatness or treacliness about fine red Burgundy, and it should charm rather than overwhelm.

On account of the way they are made, red Burgundies do mature in most years rather faster than clarets, but the finest red wines can live for many years.

Serving Burgundy It is not usual in Burgundy to decant the great red wines unless they have a marked deposit, but the British tradition is to decant so as to let the flavour and bouquet of these fine wines expand with a little aeration. The use of the exaggeratedly large glasses, urged by some chi-chi restaurants in France and Britain is, however, wholly unjustified; these goldfish bowls merely tend to over-aerate the wine, almost asphyxiate the drinker with the tremendous smell, and then give virtually nothing to the palate after the wine has crawled over an expanse of glass to the lips of the drinker.

It is probably true to say that, if one has to compare the red wines of Burgundy and Bordeaux (something wine lovers love to argue about), the finer red Burgundies are usually integral parts of a fine meal; they accompany great roasts, especially game, and any kind of meat or poultry with a wine sauce, whereas many of the finer clarets can be drunk with very simple food indeed, or even with bread and cheese.

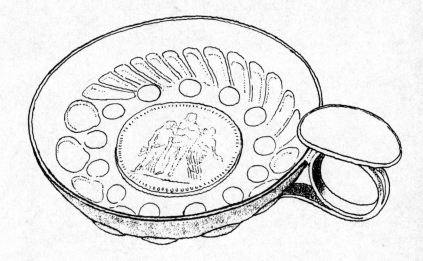

A silver tasting cup or *tastevin* used for tasting wines drawn from the cask

Other red wines

In the southern parts of the Burgundy vineyards many excellent red wines are made, which are very useful to try in these days of rising prices. Both in southern Burgundy, from just south of Beaune down to Chagny, in the **Côte Chalonnaise** and the **Mâconnais**, good everyday red wines are made in quantity nowadays. Some of the individual vineyards, such as **Monthélie, Saint-Aubin, Santenay, Saint-Romain, Mercurey** and many others are all worth trying and, if you are not insistent about getting only 'the big names', probably just as rewarding except for the greatest occasions.

Burgundy wine names The way in which wines are named in Burgundy is rather complicated. The vineyards are very much subdivided, so that a single one may have many owners, each of whom cultivates his particular patch in a slightly different way, and therefore makes a very slightly different wine. As Burgundy wines are not all estate-bottled, the man who makes the wine, the great Burgundy house or shipper, will have a further effect upon its individuality; then, when the wine is bottled, the way it is handled will make it even more of a specialized nature. This is why it is quite mistaken to say something like, 'I like Nuits-Saint-Georges' because it would be possible to put up several different Nuits-Saint-Georges wines of the same year, even in the same price range, which would be quite different from each other, according to who made the wines, handled and shipped them.

In learning Burgundy names, you should remember that the wine bearing only the name of the vineyard, such as **Corton** or **Chambertin**, is one degree up, as it were, from the wine bearing the name of the village or commune that has been made famous by those vineyards, such as **Aloxe-Corton** or **Gevrey-Chambertin**. Quite often a commune name is derived from a combination of a village and vineyard name like **Aloxe-Corton** and **Vosne-Romanée**. But sometimes the overall vineyard, such as **Chambertin**, will bear yet another vineyard name, such as **Charmes-Chambertin**, which means, usually, that the wine ranks just below that of the great vineyard, **le Chambertin**, and above that of the commune wine, **Gevrey-Chambertin**.

So the principal communes or villages of the Côte d'Or, as well as their respective vineyards, do need to be learned to choose Burgundy wisely; to help you do just that, they are given opposite.

But, as with names of people, there are no hard and fast rules for Burgundy names. For example, the white Corton Charlemagne is a finer wine than the straightforward white Corton, although, as the wine from the Corton vineyard is mostly red, the finer white wines are not difficult to remember once you have seen their names. The individually-named properties within a vineyard, such as **Les Rugiens** (Pommard), or **Les Perrières** (Fixin), are better known as sites or *climats*, which themselves may be split up between many owners. If you are buying wines with the individual site names on the label, then it is also important to know the name of the man who made the wine, or the grower, and/or the Burgundy house that bought it.

Undoubtedly Burgundy's reputation for being a difficult wine to understand emanates from its complex naming by vineyard and commune or village. When you are looking at a wine list, either of a merchant or in a restaurant maybe, make sure that you are not just buying a general vineyard wine, such as Nuits-Saint-Georges or Beaune, when you really want a more specific wine, in which case more particulars should be given after the wine's name, together with the name of the shipper if the Burgundy was not bottled on its home ground.

CÔTE DE NUITS – PRINCIPAL COMMUNES	CÔTE DE BEAUNE – PRINCIPAL COMMUNES
Red Wines	*Red Wines*
Fixin: Les Perrières and Clos du Chapître	**Aloxe-Corton**: Le Corton, Clos du Roi, and Les Bressandes
Gevrey-Chambertin: Le Chambertin, and Clos de Bèze	**Beaune**: Hospices de Beaune, Les Bressandes, and Clos des Mouches
Morey St. Denis: Clos de Tart, Clos de la Roche, part of Les Bonnes Mares, and Clos St. Denis	**Pommard**: Les Epenots, and Les Rugiens
Chambolle-Musigny: Les Musigny, and part of Les Bonnes Mares	**Volnay**: Les Caillerets
	Santenay: Les Gravières
	White Wines
Vougeot: Clos de Vougeot	**Aloxe-Corton**: Charlemagne, Le Corton-Charlemagne
Flagey-Echézeaux: Les Echézeaux, and Les Grands Echézeaux	**Meursault**: Les Perrières, Les Charmes, and Les Genevrières
Vosne-Romanée: La Romanée, La Romanée-St. Vivant, La Romanée-Conti, La Tâche, and Le Richebourg	**Puligny-Montrachet** and **Chassagne-Montrachet**: both share Le Montrachet vineyard; outstanding sites within this vineyard are Le Bâtard-Montrachet, and Le Chevalier-Montrachet
Nuits-Saint-Georges: Les Saint-Georges	

Burgundy is a wine on which it is always wise to take advice, as the ways in which it is made and marketed change very much according to different fashions in drinking and modifications and developments of legislation, as well as the policies of different firms. More than with any other wine, perhaps, it is important to have the advice of someone who knows the region and is up-to-date as regards their information.

LOIRE   The Loire region, which takes its name from the longest river in France, produces vast quantities of red and white wines, a lot of rosé and many sparkling wines, all of them, at the time of writing, still at comparatively reasonable prices. The majority appear under the names of the general vineyard sub-region or the brand of the particular house handling them, whether French or British, although some outstanding estates do export their wines under their individual labels. (For sparkling wines of the Loire *see page* 73).

Rosé wines

These are mostly made in the middle of this vineyard area in **Anjou**, and **Touraine**. They are light and medium dry, and rather pale pink in colour.

The better ones will usually bear the description *Rosé de Cabernet*, which means that they are made from the Cabernet franc grape, one of the great claret grapes and, therefore, will have a certain dryness and distinctive style.

What the wines They are very much all-purpose pink wines, but popular taste, in France as *are like* well as on the export markets, has led to many of them being made softer in style than they originally were, in order to make them a widely acceptable wine suitable for drinking with meat or fish. In some respects this is unfortunate as a medium dry, sweet pink wine is anaemic, giving very little to whatever food it accompanies, but it does mean such wines can be served with light dishes and buffet food. Otherwise, the finer rosés from the Loire are ideal partners with lightly-flavoured meat or poultry dishes and, if you wish with fish as well, including shellfish. They are, of course, suitable also for apéritifs and between-times drinking.

White wines

At the sea end of the Loire the best-known table wine is **Muscadet** (named after its grape variety), of which there are varying types and **Muscadet de Sèvre et Maine** is usually the best; there are also some single estates in the region now bottling wines under their own labels.

What the wines Muscadet is a very dry wine indeed and has become traditional as an *are like* accompaniment for shellfish as well as fish. It is best when drunk very young, but frankly it is so dry that many beginners in wine drinking cannot like it. The acidity in a Muscadet should be high, and in fact is sufficient to withstand even a sauce such as mayonnaise.

On a Muscadet label, the phrase *sur lie* means that it was bottled straight out of the cask, or in other words 'off the lees', without the wine being racked or filtered off the deposit in the cask; there may even be a tiny prickle of fermentation remaining in it, something that many people find extremely attractive in a young Muscadet.

The **Gros Plant** is another wine from this area, rather coarser and less obviously fragrant than Muscadet. It, too, can accompany fish and shellfish.

The still white wines of **Anjou, Saumur, Touraine** and, at the end of the Loire and quite near to Burgundy, those of **Pouilly-sur-Loire** and **Sancerre,** are more fruity than Muscadet, but all are dry, mostly light-bodied and can possess great elegance. Sancerre, in particular, is a wine that can have sufficient body to make it very much an all-purpose drink, either as an apéritif or to accompany fish or fairly lightly-flavoured meat dishes.

The term *Blanc Fumé* added to the label of some of the better Pouilly wines means that they have been made only from the Sauvignon blanc grape, Blanc fumé being the local name for it. The Sauvignon is now a white wine grape being used singly to make a wine of the same name in many parts of France, including Bordeaux, where it is one of the grapes used for the great white wines; it possesses an outstanding bouquet and a fairly full-bodied, lingering character.

The white wines of Anjou and Touraine are made from the grape called the Chenin blanc or Pineau de la Loire (the local name). They are a little more delicate than the wines of Pouilly and Sancerre and are capable of great variation: for example, the wines of **Vouvray** (in addition to the popular sparkling wines) can be very dry, medium or very sweet, and not only still but also *pétillant* or slightly sparkling, while the wines of the **Coteaux du Layon**, of which the most famous is **Quarts de Chaume**, can be subtly luscious and excellent with dessert fruit.

Virtually all the white wines of the Loire can be served as apéritifs, with food, or for drinks between-times, although the very sweet ones should be reserved for after meals.

Red wines

The most important red wines of the Loire are all made from one single grape, the Cabernet franc. They come from the middle of the Loire, mainly from **Touraine**, and the best-known vineyards are found around **Chinon**, **Bourgueil** and **Saint Nicolas de Bourgueil**. These red wines can be extremely charming, fruity, with a delicious light fragrance. They have, with some justification, been described as 'the Beaujolais' of the Loire; at the time of writing, they offer considerable price advantages in comparison with Beaujolais.

The red wines can accompany most meat dishes and are usually at their best when drunk fairly young. They should not be served too warm – indeed, on their home ground, they will be served, like young Beaujolais, lightly chilled or at the temperature at which they would be brought from a cool cellar, to bring out their refreshing fruitiness.

RHÔNE Along the banks of the river Rhône, from just south of Lyon down to Avignon, an enormous amount of red, white and rosé wine is produced, as well as a little sparkling wine. In the past these wines enjoyed great popularity, and the reds were highly esteemed in Britain in the 19th century; recently they have been slightly out of fashion, but now their style and their comparatively reasonable price are doing much to bring them back into favour.

The vineyards fall into three main groups: the **Côte Rôtie**, in the north of the region; those around the twin towns of **Tain-Tournon**, including **Hermitage**, **Crozes-Hermitage**, **Saint Joseph**, **Cornas**, and **Saint Péray** (renowned for its sparkling wine); then, around Avignon, there are the vineyards of **Tavel**, where the world's most famous rosé is made, **Châteauneuf-du-Pape**, **Gigondas**, **Lirac**, **Chusclan**, **Cairanne** and **Vacqueyras**. On the mountain slopes to the east the **Côtes de Ventoux** produce red and rosé wines.

It often surprises people to find that most Rhône areas produce both red and white wine, although some, such as Châteauneuf-du-Pape, are better known for their red wines. In the southern part of the region there are some great estates selling their wines under their property labels, but both here and elsewhere in the region, the wines are for the most part marketed under the name of the area, plus the name of the shipper or producer. Of course, each establishment will handle its wines in a slightly different way so that you should experiment a little before making up your mind exactly which firm produces the type of wine that you like best, but the vineyards are not subdivided as in Burgundy, and the system of naming them is by no means as complicated. Both black and white grapes are often used for the red wines, and for all the wines a large number of different grape varieties including Grenache, Syrah, and Marsanne, are permitted.

What the red wines are like

The red Rhône wines are usually of pronounced character and constituted on what might be described as a generous scale but they should not, at their best, be 'strapping', as they are sometimes described, because then they would have a coarseness that seldom pleases the discriminating lover of good wine. Most of them are fairly uncomplicated wines: easy to enjoy with regard to fragrance, which evokes sun-baked vineyards to many people, and the robust, profound flavour which, in old vintages of the finer wines, can develop subtlety, although it is not often found in the everyday ranges of Rhône wines.

These are very adaptable wines, suited for drinking with game, roasts and grills, or stews and meat pies. Their 'gutsy' style means they can partner the strongly spiced and flavoured casseroles and even salads typical of this part of the south of France. They will not be overwhelmed by the British matured cheeses, and they boost steak and kidney pie, sausage and mash, or a simple mixed grill into special company fare.

What the rosé wines are like

Tavel, the most famous rosé in the world, should be a clear bright orange-pink, with a very distinct flowery smell and a definite character; Tavel and the other rosés from this part of France (Lirac and Chusclan) are sufficiently full-bodied to partner meat dishes, as well as fish even with eggy or similar rich sauces; they are also admirable with the oily, garlicky, salads characteristic of this region. But good Tavel can never be cheap, any more than it should be nondescript, so it is by no means an all-purpose rosé.

In general, these wines are of a definite lemon-gold colour, mouth-filling in style, and dry. There are some curiosities among them, particularly the white wine of **Condrieu**, from the Côte Rôtie, which is the house wine of the great Pyramide restaurant in Vienne, and **Château Grillet**, a tiny estate in the same area, which is the only one in France to have an *appellation contrôlée* to itself. Only about 3,000 bottles of wine are made at Château Grillet even in a good year, and the wine itself is almost pinkish gold, curiously assertive, and definitely 'important'. But just because of its strange distinction it is, perhaps, like the white wine of Châteauneuf-du-Pape, a wine that few of us would find really enjoyable to drink even if it were easily found.

The white Rhônes, because of their assertive nature, are probably a little overwhelming served as apéritif wines, unless they are accompanied by very substantial snack food. But they go well with fish and some shellfish, especially any served with a rich or garlicky sauce, as their constitution prevents them from being swamped by such enemies to wine as egg yolks or piquant dressings.

Other French wines

The wines mentioned above are what are usually referred to as the classic wines of France; of course, there are many French wines. Thanks to modern developments in wine-making, what were known as 'little' wines, made solely for local consumption and which were unable to survive travel, are now enjoying wide popularity, particularly in export markets. Such wines include the wines of **Provence, Languedoc**, the **Roussillon**, the **Pyrenées**, the **Basque country**, the **Massif Central**, the **Dordogne valley**, and **Savoy**. In the **Jura** also are made the curious **vins jaunes**, or yellow wines, which slightly resemble sherry although they are not fortified; then there is the **vin de paille**, or straw wine, so named because the grapes are dried slightly on straw mats before being pressed, and **vin fou**, which is made by bottling either white or rosé wine at the peak of its first fermentation, so that it foams out of the bottle into the glass.

In Champagne there is the rather rare still white wine of the region called **Vin Nature de la Champagne**, as well as some red wines, of which the best known is **Bouzy Rouge**.

Always take the opportunity to taste a French wine from a region previously unexplored – it's an experience not to be missed. Books have been written on the well-known and lesser-known French wines, so when you are shopping for wine, if you explain you want something like a claret or like an Alsatian wine, there's no good reason why you shouldn't get something approximating to what you want.

Germany

Rhein

• Cologne

• Bonn

Koblenz

Ahr

MOSEL

Mosel

Trier

Ruwer

Saar

NAHE

Nahe

RHEINGAU

Frankfurt

Mainz

Main

FRANCONIA

Würzberg

RHEINHESSE

• Worms

PALATINATE
or PFALZ

Rhein

• Baden

Stuttgart

WURTTEMBERG

Strasbourg

BADEN

Neckar

FRANCE

• Freiburg

Bodensee

Basel

SWITZERLAND

Germany

Although some red wine is made in Germany, the majority of German wines and certainly all the finest, are white. A great deal of sparkling wine is also made, but the reputation of German wines has been founded on its still wine.

Large quantities of wine are made in the **Baden** and **Württemberg** regions, but the most famous German wines come from **Franconia** (where they are bottled in the traditional squat flagon-like Bocksbeutel) and, most important of all, from the wine regions of the **Rhine** and **Moselle** rivers and their tributaries. It is these last two areas that make the finest as well as the best-known German wines.

MOSELLE The Moselle is a beautiful river with spectacular vineyards, some of them so steep that it is difficult to maintain a footing in them, and some so terraced that there will be two or three vines on a single terrace, cultivated on the side of what is virtually a precipice. The river winds tortuously, and its constantly changing direction is the reason why the wines from two vineyards, which are virtually side by side, can be completely different in character: the outlook and the way the sun strikes the vineyards will be totally different. The **Saar** and the **Ruwer** (pronounced 'Roover') are the two tributaries of the Moselle where very fine wine is also made.

What the wines are like Good Moselle is an admirable choice for someone beginning to learn about German wines, as its delicious fragrance and crisp flavour are instantly appealing and, even among the more luscious wines, there will always be something delicate and refreshing in their character. Every wine has individual associations for the drinker, and when you are drinking a Moselle, you may find some link between the almost biting freshness of the wine and the steep, stony vineyards from which it comes, in this northern area.

Moselle can be delicious as an apéritif, or with fish, rather simple poultry dishes or cold meat; on its home ground, of course, it will be drunk with many dishes, but these are the combinations that you will probably find most acceptable. The finest wines of all are possibly enjoyed quite alone, in a room where there is no conflicting set of smells, such as strongly-perfumed flowers or people and tobacco, to detract from the wonderful bouquet of this classic wine.

THE RHINE There are four main areas producing Rhine wine: The **Rheingau**, on the north bank of the river; the **Rheinhessen**, on the west bank south of Mainz where the river turns sharply at an angle; the **Nahe**, a tributary of the Rhine, and the **Palatinate** or **Pfalz**, which is south of the Rheinhessen and to the west of the river itself. Each of these areas produces very distinctive wines, and those of the Rheingau are generally considered to be the finest examples of **hock**, the name by which wines otherwise described as Rhenish are commonly referred to.

What the wines are like It is very difficult to fit a tag description to the wines of any of these regions where there is so much variety, but it may, perhaps, be helpful to know that in general they may be described as follows:

Rheingau wines are very fine and delicate, often large-scale in style yet possessing great subtlety; usually they are rather softer in the impression they make than the Moselles.

Rheinhessen wines possess a slightly earthy flavour, which many people like a great deal, and they are the sort of wines that have made the reputation of good **Liebfraumilch**.

Nahe wines can be very flowery, with an underlying suppleness and gentle style which, in good years, can be very appealing.

Palatinate wines, made in an area which is very much everyone's idea of picturesque wine country, tend to be slightly fuller in style than the others, and, as a number of different grapes are used to make them, they may vary even more in bouquet and taste. They can, however, be surprisingly robust, and can therefore, partner many meat dishes as well as fish; some of the good regional food of the Palatinate, such as sausages, game pâtés and fine cheese, are excellent with the area's wines.

The very finest Rhine wines are probably best enjoyed alone, without food, in a fresh, clean atmosphere, but the more ordinary ones make good apéritifs, and accompaniments for shellfish and fish. With the exception of the Palatinate wines, and certain of those from the finer estates of the Rheinhessen, Rhine wines can be rather too easily swamped by meat and rich sauces for them to be served all through the meal, and the price of the finer quality wines definitely makes them 'special occasion' bottles. If you are going to combine them with other wines in the course of a meal, then the other wines ought to be red in order to be fair to both.

German wine names German wine labels often intimidate people, but they are quite easy to understand, once you adopt the habit of splitting up the long words and relating them to what they are describing, like area, vineyard, grapes and so on. For detailed explanations, *see page* 114. For all German wines sold on export markets it is essential, if you are to enjoy the experience of drinking these distinctive wines rather than simply to consume quantities of a vaguely-flavoured alcoholic beverage, to get your wines from a reputable

Some of the best German vineyards lie on steep
hillsides overlooking the river Rhine

source of supply. There's a lot of truth in the fact that, nowadays, the names of the grower and the shipper are more important, as regards German wines, than vintage dates because science has finally made it possible to make wines in years when none could formerly be made; however, only the experienced and conscientious producer and the skilled shipper will maintain the tradition of making fine wines, true to their district and vintage, and likely to make a lasting impression on the drinker.

Italy

Wine is made in nearly every region of Italy, as well as in its offshore islands of Capri, Ischia, Sardinia and Sicily, and many of the wine regions also make all kinds of wine. It should be remembered, however, that Italy is a country of very varied scenery, ranging from Alpine mountains in the north to almost desert land in the extreme south, and has only recently begun to put its wine-making on a serious commercial footing, with controls to enforce quality and to ensure a continuation of style. (For information about the Italian wine laws, *see page* 111.) When you are dealing with wines varying from very light and fresh to luscious and smooth, from delicate to full-bodied, and from sparkling or *pétillant* to dessert wines, this is a considerable achievement by any standard. Consequently, it is virtually impossible to generalize about Italian wines, although now that science has improved the way wine is made and handled, many Italian wines are far more than merely pleasant holiday drinks, and are making considerable progress in export markets. Although the wines of small firms and individual estates can be of great interest and give much pleasure, the wines handled in enormous quantities by the large well-known firms probably offer, to the inexperienced drinker, the best guarantee of getting something enjoyable.

There are so many Italian wines that space does not permit even a vaguely comprehensive list of them. But here are some of those which you may find on restaurant wine lists or in an increasing number of wine shops, with an indication as to what they are like. Remember, however, that there are many, many more, so that you should take the opportunity of trying any new to you whenever possible. Remember, too, that each of the great Italian wine firms will have a special style for their wines, so that, for example, the Chianti of one establishment may possess only a family resemblance and no close similarity to the Chianti offered for sale by another. Try several – and keep an open mind.

Red wines

Chianti: From Tuscany, this is certainly the best-known Italian red wine.

CABERNET MERLOT
TRAMINER SYLVANER
PINOT CABERNET
CABERNET MERLOT
VALPOLICELLA
SOAVE
BARDOLINO
LAMBRUSCO

AUSTRIA

SWITZERLAND

FRANCE

Bolzano
ALTO ADIGE
Lake Como
VENETO
FRIULI-
VENEZIA
GIULIA
PIEDMONT
LOMBARDY
Lake Garda
Turin
Milan
Verona
Venice
Trieste
VERMOUTH
Po
Alba · Asti
BAROLA
BARBERA
LIGURIA · Genoa
Monaco
ASTI
SPUMANTE
EMILIA ROMAGNA
· Bologna
Florence
Arno
CHIANTI
CLASSICO
Ancona
CHIANTI
Siena
THE MARSHES
VERDICCHIO
TUSCAN BIANCO
TUSCANY
UMBRIA
ADRIATIC
CORSICA
ORVIETO
Tiber
LATIUM
ABRUZZI
YUGOSLAVIA
EST EST EST
Rome
FRASCATI
CAMPANIA
APULIA
Naples
BASILICATA
LACRIMA CHRISTI
Mt. Vesuvius
SARDINIA
CALABRIA
MEDITERRANEAN
CORVO ROSSO/
CORVO BIANCO
Palermo
MARSALA
SICILY
Catania

Italy

It is available from several districts within the Chianti country, and may be non-vintage or bear a vintage date. It is a fruity wine, which can possess subtle charm, and the vintage Chiantis can be very fine. (There is no such thing as 'white Chianti' now, although white Tuscan wine of pleasant style is made.) The litre flasks are used for non-vintage Chianti, the square-shouldered claret-style bottle for the finer wines.

Barolo: Sometimes this Piedmont wine is called 'the Burgundy of Italy' but, although it is a wine constituted on a large scale, it is not really like Burgundy at all. It has an assertive smell and flavour, with great depth of taste, and is very much a wine to accompany game and great roasts.

Barbera: Markedly fruity, this is a wine that can also achieve great importance and subtlety. A vintage Barbera can be a very fine wine indeed.

Bardolino: This has been described as one of the most charming wines of Italy – a bright, lively red, with an appealing fragrance and moderate fruitiness. It is fairly light in style, and enjoyable as a luncheon wine as well as for dinner.

Valpolicella: This comes from the same region – the Veneto – as Bardolino, but it has a slightly suaver taste, and sweeter bouquet. Very easy drinking, it is enjoyable with roasts and grills, but will also partner bread and cheese.

Other red wines: Especially in the north of Italy, many wines bearing the names of classic wine grapes, such as **Cabernet**, **Pinot**, and **Merlot** are made, and all deserve trying, even though their names may not sound as glamorous as those named after Italian grapes and regions.

White wines

Soave: From the Veneto and one of the most charming of Italian wine towns, this has both fragrance and an agreeably fruity flavour.

Verdicchio is a very dry wine, with a fairly full-bodied style, usually bottled in an amphora-like bottle.

Orvieto: There are several styles of this wine, the two most frequently found being the *secco* (dry) and *abbocato* or *amabile* (rather sweet). In general, the dry wine has a fairly flowery smell and is moderately full-bodied. It is important to remember that the wicker-bound flask container used for Orvieto holds 75 cl., instead of the litre of the traditional Chianti flask.

Est! Est! Est!: This wine which can be either dry or slightly sweet, is fragrant and fresh in general style. It is bottled in the same sort of flask as Orvieto. The curious name derives from the story that, in the 12th century, a bishop on his way from Germany to Rome for the coronation of the Emperor sent his steward ahead of his route, so that the doors of the inns could be marked with an 'Est!', signifying that the local wine was good. At Monte-fiascone the steward wrote the code word three times, and he and his master remained there for the rest of their days, the bishop leaving his estate to the town and requesting that on the anniversary of his death a barrel of the wine should be poured over his grave.

Frascati: This is the best-known of the wines of the **Castelli Romani**, from a region in the Alban Hills, south-east of Rome. Dry, slightly sweet and very sweet wines are made, their colour tending to be bronze-gold, their bouquet markedly enticing.

Lacrima Christi: Both dry and sweetish versions of this wine are made around the Bay of Naples, and the name is supposed to derive from the fact that Christ, looking out of heaven at the beauty of the region, wept at the sight of so much sin on the part of man. Even the sweeter types generally display the slightly volcanic 'minerally' inner taste, for the vineyards are on the slopes around Vesuvius. Lacrima Christi is strange in that, traditionally, it is a white wine that is not supposed to be served chilled, although this is naturally a matter of personal preference.

Corvo: This is the best-known Sicilian wine at present on export markets, and there is also a red version. It is dry and light, with a slight trace of volcanic soil in the aftertaste.

Other white wines: Especially in the north of Italy, a number of wines are made simply bearing the names of the classic wine grapes making them – **Sylvaner, Traminer, Pinot Bianco** and so on.

Most Italian wines found outside Italy will be good, rather than great, unless they are from individual estates, and they are usually for immediate enjoyment instead of for putting away for long-term maturation. Wine, to an Italian, is one of the god-given pleasures of life and not something to have airs and graces about! All over the country Italians sit back and enjoy their red or white wines, regardless of whether they are eating fish or meat, and indeed most Italian wines can be enjoyed in precisely this rather informal way.

Nowadays the big bottles, litres and double litres, are becoming increasingly popular; the traditional wicker-bound litre flask is, of course, the symbol of Italian wine – especially Chianti – all over the world, although it will probably soon cease to exist, as production and labour costs have made it economically out of date. The bulbous, wicker-encased flask is the descendant of the old carafe-like type of bottle, which was used to hold wine drawn direct from the cask and then carried to the table. The wicker casing served to protect it if several flasks were hung up together at a shop or if loaded into a cart or on an animal's back for transport. Wine in wicker flasks is never meant for long keeping, and the more conventional-shaped bottles are used for wines which benefit from long-term maturation.

Spain

A huge quantity of table wine is produced in Spain – red, white and rosé, and many sparkling wines. Unfortunately, Spanish wine has earned a rather poor reputation abroad because, over a period of time, large concerns have sold the comparatively inexpensive Spanish wines under their labels with the descriptions *Spanish Burgundy*, *Spanish Chablis*, or *Spanish Claret* and so on. Other countries sometimes use the traditional generic wine names as well to describe a style of wine which in no way resembles the original other than perhaps in colour; even the sweet wines are 'sweet' in a completely different way from a genuine Sauternes. There would seem to be no justification for the maintenance of this practice and, in fact, as the public increases its knowledge and understanding of wine in its own right, many wine concerns are dropping the labelling of Spanish wines in this way.

The most important region for table wines in Spain is **Rioja**, in the northeast. Here red and white wines are made, many of them of marked quality and individuality. The whites tend to be very full in style with an extremely dry aftertaste, while the reds have what some people call the 'red earth', slightly dusty aroma and flavour of Spain – something that can be outstanding as regards quality where the estate wines are concerned.

Spain is a big country and the wines of other regions, notably that of **Valdepeñas**, where some very good white wines are made, will probably become better known as the world demand for wine increases. All are worth trying, especially if the name of the shipper is one known to enjoy a good reputation, and can be good value for money. Otherwise, you must make the experiment and take the risk.

Portugal

Wine is made up and down the length of Portugal, and it is widely agreed that at their best, the Portuguese whites tend to be superior to those of Spain, but the Portuguese reds never attain the quality of the best Spanish red wines. Nevertheless, the table wines of Portugal, sold under regional names, present both interest and real value to any drinker, and if you serve them with the right care (*see Chapter* 7), your guests probably won't have any idea what you paid for them. **Dão** wines, both red and white, are among the best

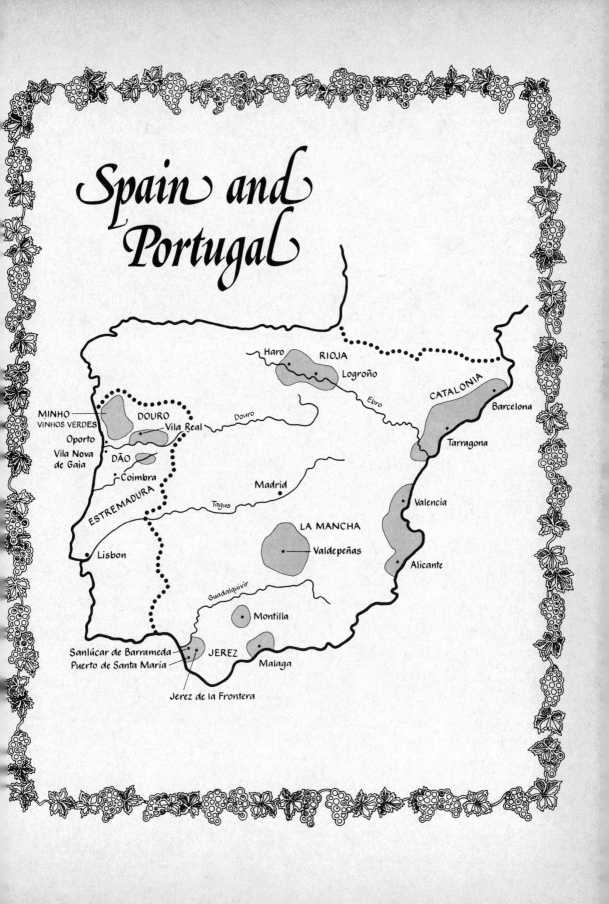

Spain and Portugal

Haro
RIOJA
Logroño
Ebro
CATALONIA
Barcelona
Tarragona
MINHO
VINHOS VERDES
DOURO
Vila Real
Douro
Oporto
Vila Nova
de Gaia
DÃO
Coimbra
Madrid
Tagus
ESTREMADURA
Valencia
LA MANCHA
Valdepeñas
Alicante
Lisbon
Guadalquivir
Montilla
Sanlúcar de Barrameda
Puerto de Santa Maria
JEREZ
Malaga
Jerez de la Frontera

known and, as regards all-purpose drinking, certainly the most useful, but there are others, such as those from the **Estremadura** region. The slightly *pétillant vinhos verdes* or 'green wines' from the **Minho** region of Portugal are described on page 680.

Mediterranean and Balkan wines

Until quite recently it would have been impossible for people who never travelled to try the wines of, for example, North Africa or the eastern Mediterranean. Wines of these countries now provide excellent everyday drinking, as well as interest for anyone on holiday there.

The Yugoslav wines, like **Lutomer riesling** and **Sylvaner**, were probably responsible for the large numbers of people in the United Kingdom beginning regular wine drinking, and it is the wines of Cyprus, the third most important source of supply for the UK, which were as much of a success with the British public after the last war as the wines of this island formerly were with the medieval crusaders and Londoners in Chaucer's time.

Hungary, Rumania, Austria, Bulgaria, Greece, the Lebanon, Tunisia, Algeria and Morocco all produce good wine, most of it generally of everyday quality, and comparatively low in price.

It is the red wines of the more southerly Mediterranean and Balkan countries which are of most interest in the northern hemisphere, because their softish, easy, fairly full style is exactly what the drinker in a cold country wants to accompany informal or family meals. The white wines from the hotter countries can be pleasant holiday drinks, but are seldom likely to be much more because the vines producing good white wines do their best in regions where there is a certain amount of cold; without the slight toughening effect of a colder climate, they tend to lack acidity and, consequently, freshness and vivacity.

Other wines of the world

Vines have been planted in parts of the United States of America, South Africa and Australia since the time of the earliest settlers, and today these countries are thoroughly established as wine producers. All types of wines are made: still and sparkling, as well as fortified, and the increased facility of transport has meant that they can be promoted and sold on markets on the other side of the world.

It is impossible to generalize about wines coming from such enormous wine regions, but those available abroad stand a fair chance of being average good to very good in quality, simply because it would not be worth while exporting them if they were not. In many instances, of course, the very finest produce of these vineyards is bound to be consumed locally, and travellers should therefore take any opportunity to try the best wines on the spot. The British system of duty, too, enables wines that come from the Commonwealth countries, such as Australia, New Zealand and Cyprus, as well as South Africa, to enjoy preferential rates of duty, so that side by side with certain European wines of a similar style, they can be cheaper; however, this must not be taken as an indication that they are inferior in quality.

As far as American wines are concerned, the main regions are New York State and California, the latter producing a very wide range of wines of all types, some of them fine by any standards in the world. American wines are not usually made from blends of different grapes and many bear the name of

Baskets of Champagne grapes stand ready for a special hand-sorting called *épluchage* so that only the perfect grapes go to the press house

the grape variety or 'varietal' from which they are made; for example, **Zinfandel** or **Cabernet Sauvignon**.

There is no legislation restricting the use of certain wine names, such as 'Champagne', outside the Common Market countries and general names such as 'hock', 'claret' and 'Burgundy' are widely used in the U.S.A., South Africa, and Australia to indicate styles of wine, just as they are in Spain.

But even if you find yourself faced with a wine list containing nothing outside the wines of these countries, you can still get an idea of what they are like by referring to the grapes from which they are made or the styles which have influenced their names and labelling. In addition, of course, an informed salesman or wine waiter should be able to give detailed counsel.

 ## *Sparkling wines*

Wines are made sparkling by three basic methods, variations on these being made by individual producers. The most obvious way of making a wine sparkling is simply to pump gas into it, but in fact 'gasified wines' are not usually of high quality. If you really want to add a suggestion of sparkle to a rather ordinary wine, it is probably best just to add soda or a similar carbonated water to it immediately before serving.

What the sparkle is   The sparkle in the two main types of good sparkling wines is a gas – carbon dioxide. When wine is made in the ordinary way, this gas is given off during fermentation but, because the wine at this stage is either in an open vat, a cask with the bung out, or simply in any large, open container, the carbon dioxide, which is naturally present, simply bursts into the air and, eventually, the wine becomes still when fermentation stops.

Some wines, while they are young, have what is often described as a 'prickle' – a quality that makes them feel 'lively', with what may be called a mini-sparkle sensation. This can be very pleasant indeed because it is refreshing – as with the Portuguese *vinhos verdes* or 'green wines' – and some of the greatest German wines and similar wines have this 'lively' characteristic, known in French as *pétillant*, in German as *spritzig*, while they are still, as it were, settling down in bottle; this is never a fault. Certain Chiantis, too, are made so that they have a very slight prickly feel in the mouth.

But the two main ways in which a wine is made sparkling are the Champagne process and that referred to as the Cuve Close or Sealed Vat method. It should be stressed that it is never worth while spending the time and skill that either of these two processes involve on a wine which is not of some quality to start with, because making a wine sparkling will show up any of its defects.

SPARKLING WINE LABELS: **1** Cristal Roederer is one of the most acclaimed De Luxe wines from the renowned Champagne house of Louis Roederer. **2** A very dry (Brut) Champagne from the famous house of Charles Heidsieck. **3** A white *vinho verde* from Portugal's Minho region. **4** A distinguished sparkling wine from Spain, made by the traditional Champagne method (*méthode champenoise*). **5** A sparkling red Burgundy from the Côte d'Or, bearing the specific *Appellation Bourgogne Mousseux*.

The best sparkling wines are made from wines that possess a certain basic acidity, which makes them fresh and crisp, and that are never very cheap. This is why the majority of the finer sparkling wines are white (although some rosé and a little red is made), and why, therefore, they tend to come from vineyards that are in the cooler part of the hemisphere, where the white wine grapes do their best on account of the cold.

The Champagne process　Technicalities can be boring and confusing but, essentially, this method means that the newly-made wine goes into bottle in the spring of the vintage after it is made, so that the second fermentation (or the end of the first fermentation, whichever you find it easiest to understand), which starts as the weather gets warmer and makes the yeasts begin working again after the winter, takes place in bottle.

The wine spends most of its life in bottle. During this time, it has any deposit that might be in it removed by the bottles being turned and shaken over a period of months, so that eventually all the 'bits' that may be in the bottle slide down to rest on the cork, which is clamped with a metal fastener onto the top of the bottle. The bottle is actually stored upside down, with this deposit on the first cork (*see illustration opposite*).

When the wine has matured sufficiently and is to be offered for sale, the first cork is skilfully removed and out comes the deposit with it. The second cork – a huge, fat mushroom-shape – goes in, is fastened down with wire, foil goes over this, the bottle is labelled and then is ready to be sold. When the first cork comes out, the bottle is topped up with more wine and any sweetening required – for some types of sparkling wine a moderate amount of sweetening goes in, for others, very little or none.

This over-simplified version of a complex process indicates some of the reasons why wines made by the Champagne method can never be cheap – too much is involved. Special bottles, as well as special corks, have to be used to resist the pressure of the gas inside the bottle (equivalent to that of a London bus tyre). The corks are more expensive than ordinary corks and, of course, these wines have to be bottled where they are made – which makes them more expensive to pack and despatch.

The important point to bear in mind is that, once such a wine goes 'on to the second cork', it will begin to age more rapidly than on the first cork. As far as **Champagne** itself is concerned, with a vintage Champagne the wine will be at its best about 7–12 or, possibly, 15 years after its vintage; old Champagne can be delightful, but many people don't like it. So there is no point in laying down such wines indefinitely. As for the non-vintage wines, which make up the bulk of all sparkling wines, including Champagne, they are ready to enjoy as soon as they are offered for sale; they won't improve in bottle and indeed shouldn't be kept for long periods.

Bottles of spark-
ling wine, made by
the *méthode champe-
noise*, are skilfully
twisted and shaken
(*remuage*) so that
the sediment
slowly slides
down onto the
corks

In France and the other E.E.C. countries, wines made by the Champagne method state this fact proudly on their labels together with the place of origin. No wine made sparkling by another method can be described just as Champagne. However, elsewhere the use of the word 'Champagne' is not protected in this way and many good wines may be described as Champagne quite legally, although they may bear little resemblance to the real thing, which is only made in the Champagne region in the north of France.

It is sensible to remember that there are plenty of good sparkling wines which should be enjoyed in their own right, and not considered as second-rate versions of Champagne. Modern techniques have ensured their quality.

The producers of the sparkling Loire wines of **Saumur** and **Vouvray**, for example, are proud of the fact that, although they were originally made fully sparkling by the Champagne method, many of the people making them went to the Champagne region after the vineyard devastation by the phylloxera pest in the late 19th century to help rehabilitate the production of quality sparkling wines.

The Cuve Close method This process, evolved by a Monsieur Charmat (whose name is often used for it), virtually follows the Champagne process, but the wine undergoes its final fermentation and maturation in a sealed vat instead of a bottle. It has been found very suitable to apply to wines which are at their best when drunk young, so that the long period of maturation in bottle and the processes involved with handling them, can be shortened; the labour involved is not so great, and all these savings result in an eventual saving on the price paid by the customer. Very few of the wines made sparkling by this method bear vintage dates, as they are at their best as soon as they are offered for sale, so there is no point whatever in putting them aside for further maturation.

The wines shed their deposit in the vat; later they are bottled under pressure so that they do not lose their sparkle. For many of them nowadays – and for some Champagnes – plastic stoppers are used, instead of corks, but even so they can never be cheap wines.

There are many variations on the Cuve Close method, including one much used in the U.S.A. and Australia, whereby the wine is matured in bottle at the beginning of its life, then decanted into a sealed vat and rebottled; usually the label will state 'matured in bottle'. Most **Asti Spumante**, one of the great sparkling wines of Italy, is made by a process that combines the two methods. Most of the German **sekt** or sparkling wine is made by the Cuve Close method.

But it should always be remembered that a good sparkling wine, wherever it comes from and however it is made, should be appraised for its own quality, not as an imitation of anything else. The wine that makes a good sparkling wine must be good, and this is one of the reasons why sparkling wines are often recommended in cases of convalescence or to revive energy or appetite; it is also why it is said, with some truth, that 'there isn't a single headache' in a bottle of quality sparkling wine.

Types of sparkling wines Most establishments making sparkling wines will produce several types: usually dry or medium dry, and slightly or definitely sweet. Very sweet sparkling wines have fallen slightly out of fashion, but in fact they are most enjoyable at the end of a meal – perhaps for a toast on a birthday – or even as an apéritif, if people feel rather tired.

The term *blanc de blancs* simply means that the wine has been made wholly from white grapes; most Champagne is made from both black and white grapes. The term is not confined to sparkling wines, but Champagne of this type is very light and elegant, although certainly not always the ideal, anytime and all-purpose Champagne. The black Pinot grapes in Champagne give the wine its bouquet and fruitiness.

Some Champagne establishments make luxury or **De Luxe** wines, from a selection of their finest *cuvées* or vattings, which are definitely very special occasion wines; among the best-known are Dom Pérignon, Dom Ruinart, La Grande Dame, Chasteau de Irroy, Comte de Champagne, Diamant Bleu, Belle Epoque, and Roederer Cristal. **Vintage Champagne** will possess the character of the individual vintage year. **Pink Champagne** is made either by allowing a little colour from the black grapes into the must during the pressing or by blending a quantity of still red wine from the Champagne region into the *cuvée*.

The term *vin mousseux* is applied to all French sparkling wines, including, of course, Champagne – but not all *vins mousseux* are Champagne! Champagne is also the only fine wine of France that is legally allowed simply to bear on its label the phrase *vin de Champagne*, without an *appellation contrôlée*. The still wine of Champagne, *Vin Nature de la Champagne*, is comparatively rare, and always expensive, because obviously it is better business for the firms to sell their sparkling wine, and they do not want to risk having any unscrupulous person gasifying the still wine and selling it as 'Champagne'.

Some famous names Sparkling wines are usually sold by the name of the house or firm producing them, plus the region from which they come. In Champagne, the *Grandes Marques* or most famous houses are: Ayala, Bollinger, Clicquot-Ponsardin, Heidsieck Monopole, Charles Heidsieck, Irroy, Krug, Lanson, Mercier, Moët et Chandon, G. H. Mumm, Perrier-Jouët, Piper Heidsieck, Pol Roger, Pommery et Greno, Louis Roederer, Ruinart, and Taittinger. There are many other excellent establishments, some of them making wines to be labelled B.O.B. (Buyer's Own Brand) for certain wine merchants and important restaurants. For example, at the time of writing the house Champagne of the Savoy Group in London is that of the very large and respected Champagne establishment of De Venoge.

Other famous French sparkling wines come from **Vouvray**, where they may be slightly or fully sparkling, dry or sweetish; from **Saumur**, where they are mostly dry or medium-dry; these wines are made by the Champagne process, as are many other increasingly popular sparkling wines from **Touraine**. The Charmat firm make **Veuve du Vernay**, from a blend of wines from various regions; **Blanquette de Limoux**, from the south-east,

Seyssel from the east, and the various types of sparkling **white Burgundy**, some sparkling **red Burgundy**, and sparkling **white Beaujolais** are made by several firms; the **Vin Fou** of the Jura is made by the firm of Henri Maire of Arbois, and a sparkling **Alsace** is made by the Champagne method by Dopff & Irion, and some other wines are also made in Alsace by the Cuve Close method.

In Italy, the most famous sparkling wine is white **Asti**, made in Piedmont by numerous firms; made from the Muscat grape, it is a very fruity wine with a pronounced bouquet. Some other sparkling wines are made from the white Pinot chardonnay grape, and are dryer. The curious red sparkling wine, **Lambrusco**, from Emilia-Romagna, is fruity but very dry; traditionally, it is good with many of the rich dishes of Bologna, a centre of Italian gastronomy, and is especially admirable with zampone (stuffed pig's trotters).

In the north of Spain there are several huge concerns making sparkling wines, much of it produced by the Champagne method. In Portugal, the Real Vinicola do Portugal make a sparkling wine by this method.

In Germany many firms produce **sekt**, the largest being Henkell; this is a wine made from a blend of selected wines. Other firms, such as Deinhard, make sparkling **hock** and **Moselle**, Sichel make a sparkling **Liebfraumilch** and there are many others, most of them making use of the Cuve Close method, but a few actually employing the Champagne method.

The sparkling **Edelperl** of Luxembourg is becoming known abroad, and in many of the Eastern European countries sparkling wines are made, although not many appear on the lists of countries outside their borders. A quantity of sparkling wine is made in the U.S.S.R., much of it being rather sweet, but again, not much appears on export markets. Around the Mediterranean most countries producing white wines also make some sparkling wine, but this seldom achieves more than moderate quality.

In Australia a number of sparkling wines are made, also the **perl** wines which are slightly sparkling. In South Africa, too, sparkling wines of good quality are made.

In the U.S.A., the best-known sparkling wine is undoubtedly that of **Great Western**, in New York State, but in California and increasingly throughout all the wine regions of the U.S.A., sparkling wines are made by various processes. They can achieve notable quality, because certain of the white wines on which they are based are exactly the type to make fine sparkling wines. In the Napa Valley, for example, the **Schramsberg Champagne** is made from the Champagne grapes, Pinot noir and Pinot chardonnay, and has achieved fame according to the reports by authorities on European wines. American sparkling wines labelled as being made by 'Bulk Process' mean that they have been produced by the Cuve Close or Charmat method; if the label says 'fermented in *this* bottle', the wine will probably have been made by the Champagne process. A label stating 'fermented in bottle' implies a wine that has been fermented in a bottle, then emptied, the sediment filtered out and the wine rebottled under pressure, thereby remaining sparkling.

Fortified wines

Fortified wines are made in many wine regions, but the most famous are **Sherry**, **Port**, **Madeira** and **Marsala**. Strict legislation protects the use of these names in Europe, so that port can come only from Portugal, and sherry from the Sherry region in the south-west of Spain. U.S.A. regulations also require that the label of such wines should indicate their origins.

Madeira, made on the island of that name, is produced by a method that seems to be unique in wine-making and has not been imitated in quite the same way. Marsala, the other great classic fortified wine and made in southern Sicily, is also distinctive in style and has not been imitated in the same way as port and sherry.

Port and sherry

—how they are made Both wines start from pressed grape juice, the grapes and the method whereby they are crushed being carefully controlled, as is the exact area within which they may be grown. The port region is on the banks of the upper part of the River Douro in north Portugal (*see map on page 65*); the sherry region lies in the south-west of Spain (*see map on page 65*) around the towns of Jerez de la Frontera, Puerto de Santa Maria, and Sanlúcar de Barrameda, which is actually on the sea.

The basic difference between these two great classic wines is that, whereas sherry is allowed to complete its fermentation, so that all the grape sugar is converted into alcohol to give a bone-dry wine, the fermentation of port is arrested at a precise moment by the addition of brandy, which makes it impossible for the yeasts to go on working. This does not mean that port is a sweet wine, but there is always a certain inner sweetness in port which has made it so popular in all the northern or cold countries.

Sherry, on the other hand, receives any sweetening required by the addition of sweet wine after fermentation; this is necessary in order to make the styles of sherry which appeal to various export markets, again, mostly, those where the climate is cold and damp. Sweet sherry is not drunk in Spain, and in fact you might find it hard to get a bottle even in the sherry region itself.

Types of sherry

Sherry spends most of its life in huge casks or butts, kept in *bodegas*, the vast above-ground stores of wine, which are likened to cathedrals because of the pillars between which the sherry butts are stacked in long aisles, and the hushed, cool atmosphere. In these *bodegas* are maintained the *solera* or scale of wines from which the particular blend of the establishment is made up. It is possible to blend various types of sherry from different sources together, and many good everyday types are produced in this way, but straight *solera* wines are those which live their lives in this single set of casks, the wine being drawn off in different proportions from the different casks as it is required, so that the result is, as it were, a very special type of sherry, of individual character. There is no such thing as a vintage sherry, although some sherry labels bear the date indicating when the *solera* from which they come was first laid down. In all fine sherry there will be a proportion of very old precious wine. Each one of the great sherry houses will make a very wide range of wines, at varying prices, to suit different markets and occasions. There will, for example, be an inexpensive fino as well as a rather costly one, and, if you are comparing the wines of different sherry producers, it is not fair to appraise the cheap wine of one house alongside the expensive one of another – try to choose them within the same price range. But all will bear the individual stamp of the house that is responsible for them.

Fino: This is the driest type of sherry, varying from pale gold to almost

A typical bodega or sherry cellar with a solera of wines

grapefruit-gold in colour. This type of sherry can be very dry indeed, some people finding certain wonderful finos really too palate-scrapingly dry for their taste, but there are other good finos which have had a very slight sweetening for them to appeal to certain markets. Essentially, though, fino is a bone-dry wine. It should always be served chilled and it will deteriorate once the bottle has been opened four or five days. The charm of fino is its beautiful freshness and lovely fragrance (which is why you should never fill a sherry glass to more than one-half or two-thirds) and exposure to the air, in an opened bottle or decanter, will quickly deprive you of this pleasure.

Manzanilla is a special type of fino, also bone-dry, but made and matured only at Sanlúcar de Barrameda, near the sea, so that some people find a salty flavour in this style of wine. Both these types of sherry are admirable apéritifs, and can also accompany shellfish and what might be described as 'savoury nibbles' by way of snacks.

In Spain very copious snacks called *tapas* are frequently offered with sherry for some time before a meal. The traditional way of serving sherry was to put a biscuit across the top of the glass, like a lid or cover, to prevent any dust falling into the wine; this Victorian custom is still sometimes followed in London bars.

Amontillado: This, at its finest, is what may be described as a matured fino: it has aged in wood, so that its first youthful freshness has gone and a beautiful supple style has developed, together with an intensely-fragrant smell and a flavour that reminds some people of nuts. It is deep golden in colour with a touch of tawny brown about it. But amontillado of this kind is an expensive wine and what many people enjoy as a 'medium sherry' in both the price and style sense of the words is an amontillado-type derived from blending certain types of sherry to approximate to this particular style. There is nothing the matter with this if you enjoy the wine.

If you serve an amontillado as an apéritif, then it too should be chilled like fino so that the pleasant bouquet and flavour are, as it were, polished up. An amontillado is also the type of sherry to serve with clear consommé and, indeed, the perfect all-purpose sherry if you suppose people to whom you are offering a casual drink do not care for a truly bone-dry wine, or if you yourself want something that is a little softer in style than a fino without being definitely sweet.

Oloroso is a soft, rather assertively fragrant, golden-tawny sherry; in the top price ranges, it can be a most beautiful wine, big and supple, without necessarily being sweet at all. Indeed, it should not be a sweet wine but, again to suit market requirements in cold countries, many olorosos are on the sweet side.

In Jerez, the *venencia*, made of whalebone and with a silver cup at one end, is the traditional instrument used for drawing wines from sherry butts

Sweet sherries: These very often bear names including the words 'milk' or 'cream'. The port of Bristol, famous for the sherries it shipped, has been handling **Bristol Milk** since the time of Samuel Pepys; the most famous cream sherry of all, **Bristol Cream**, is the brand name of John Harvey, the use of which dates from the end of the 19th century when a lady visitor to their premises was shown a very fine oloroso described as Bristol Milk, and then a still finer wine, at which she exclaimed, 'If that be milk, this must be cream!'.

These sherries are usually dark brown, luscious and velvety in style; they tend to be sweet or very sweet, but it is worth noting that the very old wine on which they are founded is not necessarily sweet at all and, therefore, there should never be anything cloying about fine sherry in this category. The inexpensive sweet sherries, of course, appeal because of their sweetness.

Sweet sherries are wines which can be served at virtually any time, although if you want to drink them before or at the beginning of a meal, remember that they can, in the top ranges, be rather overwhelming and, therefore, may overshadow any wine that is to follow them immediately. Ideally, they are between-times wines or for drinking with dessert fruit and nuts. Some people like them lightly chilled, and there has been a successful advertising campaign to drink these sweet sherries 'on the rocks', but diluting a fine wine with ice cubes seems rather a shame – better to put the bottle in the refrigerator or ice bucket and cool it that way.

Serving sherry Always serve sherry in a goblet or tulip-shaped glass, never pouring the wine to more than half or at most two-thirds of the way up the glass. This enables the beautiful smell to be enjoyed. The glasses often described as sherry glasses, such as the waisted Elgin, the thistle glass, and the tiny inverted triangles sometimes used for apéritifs, do much to deprive you of any enjoyment of this great classic wine.

Sherry is one of the very few wines that can withstand cigarette or even cigar smoke – why this should be so is a mystery but, if correctly served, it can be enjoyed almost anywhere and at any time, and indeed in the sherry region people will drink it happily all through a meal.

Sherry-style wines Many countries today make a wine following what might be described as the sherry procedure. The most notable of these is Cyprus, which supplies one-third of the U.K.'s wines at the time of writing. South Africa and Australia also make wines of this kind, and British sherry, made from either de-hydrated grapes which are reconstituted in the U.K., or imported unfermented must, have played an important part in introducing many people to wine drinking for the first time. Many people think that because these wines are cheap, they are therefore less good but, in fact, those coming from Cyprus, South Africa and Australia have, up to the present time, enjoyed a preferential rate of duty, which means they can be sold on the British market at a much lower price than the equivalent type of wine from other countries, therefore the price does not directly reflect the quality of the wine.

What is important is that all these wines should be appraised and enjoyed as fortified wines in their own right – it may be of interest to compare them with sherry, but it is not really very sensible to do this. The grapes, the climate, their detailed methods of production are all different and, therefore, the wine is bound to be different. The essential is that it should be enjoyed.

Types of port

Port has, justly, the reputation of having been virtually created for the British market, but it is immensely popular throughout the world today, especially in France and Denmark. It is a wine that may be enjoyed at many times of day, quite outside the context of meals, and there are many interesting traditions associated with it – for example, the health of the British sovereign is traditionally drunk in port on occasions such as the sovereign's birthday, or at Christmas. Although it is often referred to as 'the Englishman's wine', in fact many of the great port shippers are of Scottish origin. But there are Portuguese port houses as well, and the range of wines produced by each port establishment will bear the individuality of that house.

White port: This is made entirely from white grapes, is slightly dry in style and a lemony-gold in colour. Chilled, it is admirable as an apéritif.

Ruby port is a deep and bright red. Essentially, this is young port, very much an anytime drink, which may be enjoyed between-times or at the end of a meal. Before the 1914–18 war, it was the popular wine by the glass in many pubs, and is just the warming drink to have on a cold winter night.

Tawny port can be either a very fine old matured port, which started life as a ruby, or else, in the cheaper ranges, a blend of ruby port and an older wine. It is usually a beautiful brownish gold colour, with a complex lingering bouquet and, at its finest, has a fascinating flavour. The best type of tawny port is the sort that the shippers themselves enjoy drinking after luncheon, both in Oporto and Britain, and the gentle subtlety of this wine makes it a wonderful finish to a meal, without any complications re-garding decanting. You can also drink it between-times, if you wish, and it is a particularly good wine to offer to anyone who comes in during the evening, whom you wish to honour.

White, ruby and tawny ports are matured in wood casks or 'pipes' and are ready to enjoy as soon as they go into bottle – there is no sense in putting them away.

Keeping white,
ruby and
tawny ports

These may all be left in the bottle or decanter in a cool place after they have been opened for a few days without deterioration, although after about a week their smell and subtle flavour will decline. You need not decant any of these types of port unless you wish, but certainly the beautiful colour of any port is best displayed in a fine decanter or carafe. Be careful that the glass for port is not too small – most glasses sold as port glasses are on the minute side. Port goes very well with all forms of dessert fruit and nuts, you can put a little into a chilled melon at the beginning of a meal, if you wish, or serve it with the first course.

Vintage port is a unique style of port. Each house shipping port will decide whether or not to declare a vintage when a particularly fine style of port seems to have been made, and this port, unlike all others, will spend most of its life in bottle.

Vintage port is bottled two or three years after its vintage date and spends the rest of its life in that bottle; usually it is not ready to drink at all until it is 8–10 years old, a good or great vintage should certainly not be drunk until it is 15–20 years old and it can go on improving for many years after that. This

PLATE 1: Château Ausone is one of the outstanding vineyard properties in St. Emilion – a district whose red wines make an ideal introduction to claret drinking

PLATES 2 AND 3: *Two of the best-known wine districts of the Rhône valley are Châteauneuf-du-Pape* (above), *whose pebble-strewn vineyards are typical of the area, and Tavel* (left), *the source of the world's most famous rosè wine.*

wine used to be a speciality of the United Kingdom and was always bottled here, either by the representative of the shipper, or a merchant; in recent years, however, there has been an increasing tendency for shippers to bottle their own port, and nowadays Portuguese-bottled vintage port is also a usual thing. As with table wines, it is generally true that Portuguese-bottled port tends to mature a little faster than port bottled and matured in the colder, damper climate of the British Isles, but there should be no foolish snobbery about one necessarily being better than the other.

Vintage port forms a crust or type of deposit on which the wine virtually lives during its life in the bottle. It is important that this crust should be allowed to form when the wine goes into bottle, and therefore ideally the bottle should not be disturbed, at least for the first five years of the wine's life. A white splash of paint on the bottle will indicate how the bottle has originally been binned or stored, so that if it has to be moved, the deposit can still be encouraged to reform on the underside, away from the splash. If you have to move vintage port after five years or so it is quite possible for the crust to reform after some weeks or months, even if it has been considerably shaken up, but initially the wine should be left alone as much as possible.

At any time, when you are serving vintage port, the crust should not be

A picturesque *barco rabelo*, formerly used to bring pipes of port down from the Douro vineyards to the port lodges at Vila Nova de Gaia

allowed to affect the wine. This means that, again, ideally, the bottle must be undisturbed for some weeks before it is to be opened, during which time it should stand up to let the deposit slip down the bottle. It can then be decanted, so that the wine is poured off the deposit and is bright and clear. A wine merchant will always decant a vintage port for you given notice, putting it either into a decanter or into a clean wine bottle which can then be corked up, so that you can take it home and transfer it to your own decanter.

Vintage port is a wonderful wine and very much a drink with which to finish a meal served on a special occasion. Every port house has its own style, and every vintage has its own individuality, so that trying and comparing these can be an almost infinite pleasure. Vintage port should be drunk within 24 hours of the bottle being decanted and preferably at a single session.

Lage-bottled vintage: This is a style of port evolved especially to accord with the demands of contemporary drinking; it is the wine of a single vintage year, but it spends five or six years in the cask before being bottled. So essentially it begins life as a young ruby and then, in the cask, it grows the deposit on which it lives; then, when it is bottled, this deposit is left behind. Thus the wine has the characteristics of a vintage port yet needs no decanting, for it is perfectly clear and can be poured out to the last drop. It is generally rather lighter in both colour and body than a vintage port, but is a noble wine and deserves reserving for a fairly special occasion at least.

One of the most famous ports of this kind is the **Noval**, which was pioneered by the late owner of Quinta do Noval, Luiz Porto. He foresaw the necessity for those who wanted to drink port to be able to do so easily, without bothering to decant it, and who also might have to keep a bottle of fine port in a centrally-heated house or flat. This is the way certain Noval ports, including their Noval late-bottled, were evolved.

Crusted port: This is another port catering for the requirements of the drinker of today. It is usually a blend of good wine from several years, which is allowed to mature in wood for longer than usual if it were going to be bottled as a vintage, perhaps up to five years; it is then bottled, where it throws or forms a crust – hence its name – and assumes some of the characteristics of vintage port, including the beautiful smell and vigorous, aristocratic style. Each port house will follow its own practices with regard to crusted port, Noval's, for example, being always the wine of a single year, whereas other good houses will blend their crusted port from other years.

You must, of course, decant the wine off its crust before serving it, but the fact that this type of port matures more quickly than a vintage port enables people to enjoy wines of a vintage style without having to wait for 15–20 years to do so. It is also, obviously, less expensive.

FORTIFIED WINE LABELS: **1** Most Madeiras are sold under brand names, like Old Trinity House Bual from the well-known firm of Rutherford & Miles. **2** White port, made entirely from white grapes, is one of many port styles emanating from the towns of Oporto and Vila Nova da Gaia on the mouth of the Douro river, which date from the early 18th century as centres of the port trade. Three different styles of Spanish sherry: Manzanilla (**3**), a more luscious, sweet Oloroso type (**4**), and bone-dry Fino (**5**).

Other ports   **Estate wines:** In general, port is made from wines coming from different vineyards, and a number of grapes are involved in its production. But there are a few single estates, called *quintas* (Quinta do Noval being, perhaps, the most famous of all), and certain of these estate wines are occasionally seen on wine merchants' lists. These have great individuality and, because the wine made from them is naturally limited, tend to be expensive.

Nacional wines: The term *Nacional* is also seen on some port labels. This, of which the Noval estate also provides what is possibly the best-known example, will never be seen on a commercially-available wine, because the term means that the grapes have been grown on national or original vine stocks, which have not been grafted. The phylloxera pest is still present in the soil of the Douro valley, so great care and attention have to be devoted to these vines to enable them to survive at all, but the type of port made from them, as compared with the port made from vines grafted on to American stocks, which are resistant to the phylloxera, is rather different in style, softer and, some people think, subtler. To taste a nacional port is to enjoy a memorable experience.

Port-style   Wines made following a procedure similar to that observed in the production
wines   of port may be found in certain vineyards throughout the world, and they can give pleasure to those who want a full-bodied drink of soft flavour but fairly assertive style. It is probably not unfair to say, however, that, whereas the adoption of the sherry method of production has resulted in a number of wines of high quality, the emulation of the port procedure has hardly ever resulted in wines that are more than average. Maybe the future will give the lie to this.

Madeira

Types of   Madeira is an easy wine to learn about, because it comes from the island of
Madeira   the same name, which belongs to Portugal, and there are four main types, each one named after the grape from which it is made.

Sercial is the driest wine and lightest in colour, suitable for serving either as an apéritif or with certain types of first course, or it can be drunk virtually at any time. You may chill it, if you wish.

Verdelho: This is a slightly darker-coloured Madeira, also softer in style without being in the least sweet, and has an aroma and flavour that remind some people of nuts. This, too, is an any time drink, which may be served lightly chilled before a meal and, like sercial, may accompany a clear consommé or certain straightforward fish dishes.

Bual, or in Portuguese *Boal*: This is a very velvety, deep golden-brown wine, verging towards sweet, and suitable for drinking between-times and particularly with dessert fruit and nuts at the end of a meal.

Malmsey is the greatest dessert Madeira, deep brown in colour and velvety in texture. It has a wonderful fragrance, without being in the least cloying or over-assertive, and it is the supreme wine to enjoy either quite by itself after a good meal, or simply with some fruit and nuts.

Both Malmsey and Bual can also be enjoyed with the simpler type of fruity pudding, or a piece of cake, if you wish to serve them outside the context of a meal, and either a plain sponge cake or a sweetish biscuit is acceptable with all types – Madeira was the traditional refreshment given to an important customer of a solicitor or bank prior to 1914. It possesses the great advantage that, in addition to remaining in good condition for drinking for a week or more after the bottle or decanter is opened (you need not decant Madeira, but the beautiful colour is shown off well in a handsome decanter with a stopper), the wine can be enjoyed without being chilled, even the dryer types. It is, therefore, a very easy wine to serve, and it fits well into the scheme of present-day drinking, so that it is not surprising that it is beginning to enjoy a revival in fashion. In the U.S.A. Madeira has always been popular as, in the early days of the independence of the American colonies, the island sent enormous quantities to North America.

There is no such thing as a vintage Madeira nowadays, although occasionally vintage wines can be found – some of them very old indeed, as Madeira has the reputation (disputed by sherry) of being the longest-lived wine in the world. Eighteenth century Madeiras are still to be drunk on great occasions if you are a guest of a Madeira shipper.

There are no single estate Madeiras, but a few firms do produce blends, combining the different grapes. **Rainwater** is one of the best-known of these, from the firm of Cossart Gordon, but the bulk of Madeira is made from single grape varieties.

Marsala

Marsala is not very fashionable today, except among the Italians who make it, and in Italian communities overseas. But it is a versatile wine and may very well come back into fashion. It was, in fact, evolved by three Britons, in the town from which it takes its name, and it enjoyed enormous popularity in Britain in the 19th century.

Types of Marsala   It may surprise people, who only associate Marsala with the **sweet variety**, used for making zabaglione, to learn that there are **dry Marsalas**, others flavoured with **almonds** and various types of **fruit** and, of course, there is

Marsala all'uovo, which is Marsala enriched with egg yolks to make a particularly rich, sweet drink.

Dry Marsala can be served as an apéritif or with certain first courses; the sweeter types are good with dessert fruit and nuts, and, because of the slightly 'roasted' or 'minerally' flavour, which this particular wine possesses, it can partner various puddings without being overwhelmed by strong flavours, such as those of orange, which tend to swamp more delicate dessert wines.

Some names to remember

It is obviously impossible to list all the producers of sherry, port, Madeira and Marsala, let alone their most famous brands. Many firms sell most of their wines to export markets and are comparatively little-known in the region of production; with others the reverse is true. Even with those firms whose names are world-famous, certain lines may be produced for specific export markets, which are either quite different from those wines made for consumption on their home ground, or else the wines may bear different names, according to where they are to be sold.

Some wine merchants, too, will have a wine specially blended for their particular clientele and put their own name on the label, so that personal preferences can be established only by trying a variety of wines and remembering those you like and those you do not find to your taste. Sometimes a merchant's fortified wine will, simply because it doesn't have to bear heavy advertising costs, be cheaper than a nationally – or internationally – advertised brand, but it need in no way be inferior.

In preparing this short list of some of the better-known shippers, their names have been given in the form in which they are likely to be most familiar or most easily recognized; wines made according to the styles of the classic fortified wines and coming from other parts of the world are not included, but usually their labels indicate their style and, for travellers, someone on the spot should be able to recommend a good firm and brand.

Sherry **At Jerez:** Bertola, Blazquez, Chaves y González, Croft, Díaz Morales, Diez Hermanos, Garvey, González Byass, Guerrero Ortega, Hidalgo, José Martinez, Luis G. Gordon, Lustau, Mackenzie, Manuel Fernández, Manuel Guerrero, Marqués del Mérito, Marqués del Real Tesoro, Marqués de Misa, Muñoz, Pedro Domecq, Pemartín, La Riva, Ruíz-Mateos, Sánchez Romate, Sandeman, Valdespino, Williams & Humbert, and Wisdom & Warter.

At Puerto de Santa Maria, Sanlúcar de Barrameda, and **Cadiz:** Cuvillo, Duff Gordon, Jiménez, Jiménez Varela, Luis Caballero, Osborne,

Terry, Ximénez, Barbadillo, Enrique Gutierrez Renero, Lacave, Pedro Romero, Sánchez Ayala, Vinícula Hidalgo.

Port Whereas in the sherry region each great establishment preserves its own individuality, albeit it is still making sherry, there is somewhat of a distinction between the British port houses and the Portuguese port establishments. Some people might say, with a certain justification, that the Portuguese port establishments make a style of wine that is generally a little softer and more easy-going, as might be expected from a port made to be consumed in warm countries; certain other port houses, however, bearing names which indicate their northern origin, make wines to appeal to specific export markets.

Although it is the British shippers that have made the reputation of port throughout the world, the appeal and charm of the admirable wines made by the Portuguese houses should never be overlooked, as is sometimes rather ungraciously done in books devoted to this great wine. Names are as follows: Borges & Irmao, Burmester, Calem, Cockburn Martinez, Croft, da Silva, Delaforce, Diez Hermanos, Ferreira, González Byass, Graham, Hunt Roope, Kopke, Mackenzie, Manuel Misa, Offley Forester, Pinto, Real, Real Companhia Vinicola, Robertson, Sandeman, Serra, Silva & Cosens, Smith

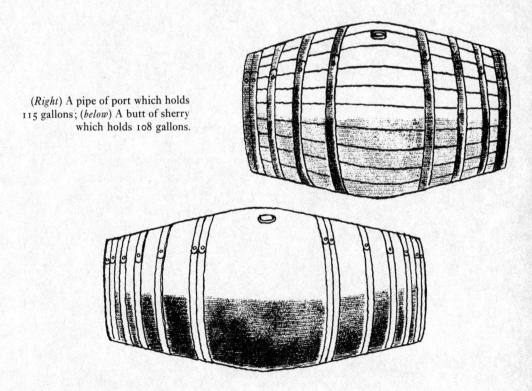

(*Right*) A pipe of port which holds 115 gallons; (*below*) A butt of sherry which holds 108 gallons.

Woodhouse, Taylor Fladgate & Yeatman, Valenta Costa, Warre, Wiese & Krohn.

Firms such as John Harvey, Croft, Sandeman, and Mackenzie, have large establishments in both the sherry and port regions, and many of the large wine concerns in the United Kingdom are associated with at least one important sherry *bodega* or port lodge, so as to have constant and exclusive supplies of these basic classic wines.

Madeira   The Madeira Wine Association, with its headquarters in Funchal, numbers among its members many very well-known Madeira establishments, but it should be stressed that the wine of each of these houses retains its individuality, as regards all the Madeiras that it produces. There are also many excellent Madeiras made by firms who are not members of the Association. Names are as follows: Barbeito, Blandy, Borges, Cossart Gordon, Gerraz, Freitas Martins Caldeira, Enriques & Enriques, Kopke, Litoq, Luiz Gomez, Rutherford & Miles, Shortridge Lawton.

Marsala   The Marsala establishments best known throughout the English-speaking world are those of Woodhouse, Ingham, and Whitaker, and today all three are owned by the Florio establishment, itself belonging to Cinzano. There are, however, a number of other excellent producers of Marsala in that town, including Carlo Pellegrino (nothing to do with the mineral water San Pellegrino); wines made by firms, which may sell vast quantities among Italian communities, should be tried (whenever possible) by anyone liking this style of wine.

Vermouth

Any wine country can make a vermouth, but the most important, commercially, are those of France and Italy, where vermouth is very big business. Production started there in regions where there was an abundance of wine suitable to the vermouth process, as well as many herbs from the mountains and spices with which to flavour it. Turin, in Italy, Marseilles in the south of France, and Chambéry in the north-east of France, are the main vermouth centres.

Types of vermouth   It is not true, as many people suppose, that Italian vermouth is sweet and French is dry. Each one of the firms making vermouth, many of which have establishments in both Marseilles and Turin, now produce a complete range of drinks, including the increasingly popular **bianco** or white vermouth, which is only made in Italy. French vermouth is generally made in a slightly different way from Italian, but this is something that need not concern us here. The sweet vermouths are usually darkish-red or reddish-brown in colour, the dry vermouths pale or yellow-gold. The bianco type is usually on the sweet side compared with ordinary dry vermouth. The vermouths of **Chambéry** are very light in colour with an extremely pleasant herby smell and fresh, delicate flavour.

Different brands of vermouth will taste different, so it's up to you to decide which you prefer. However, vermouth is very much a refreshing drink, whether it is drunk straight or made into a long drink with carbonated water, or whether it forms part of a mixed drink, such as dry and sweet vermouth mixed, or vermouth cassis (dry vermouth with a spoonful of cassis liqueur). It may be drunk at virtually any time but, because of its freshness (which is true even of the sweeter types), it is particularly good as an apéritif and, of course, being essentially a wine, it can be served before fine wines. Vermouth can also be made into a long drink and spun out over a period of time, should there be no ordinary table wine offered as an alternative to a stronger drink on such occasions.

Vermouth, incidentally, is a very good 'when in doubt' occasional drink, because it is widely available, is only a little higher in alcoholic strength than table wine, and is also a useful alternative to spirits or the sweeter fortified wines for anyone slimming.

As vermouth is a wine, opened bottles must not be simply kept in the cupboard and expected to last for ever! Indeed, the dry light vermouths deteriorate markedly after a fortnight and, although it will do you no harm if you drink them, they may taste unpleasant. It is always better to use up any drainings of vermouth in the kitchen, where it is a most valuable ingredient in many sauces and stocks (because of the ingredients that flavour it so subtly). Sweet vermouth, and bianco too, can be kept, once opened, for longer than white, but even so about a month is as long as it is likely to remain in a palatable condition. Ideally, vermouth should be kept in a cool place. You can keep a bottle in a refrigerator, putting it in the least cold part, and this will prolong the life of the wine.

Famous names The following are only a few of the many vermouths internationally available. It should also be appreciated that many retailers of wine have their own house brands of vermouth made up for them.

Chambéry: Gaudin, Dolin.
Italian and French: Martini & Rossi, Noilly Prat, Cinzano, Bosca, and Riccadonna.
British vermouth: this is made subject to strict controls by Vine Products and marketed under the brand name of Votrix.

Chapter 4 *Appreciating Wine*

There is only one way to find out what a wine is like – buy a bottle, draw the cork and taste it! Learning to appreciate wine isn't so much difficult as time-consuming, and it would take more than any one person's lifetime to know all there is to know about one wine.

If only there were not so many different types of wine, it would be possible to give a few definite recommendations for wines suitable for certain occasions and people could simply go to the shop and buy the appropriate bottle. But no one wine merchant, however distinguished, can stock every single wine to suit every potential customer and this is where the customer must show a little practical intelligence. After all, you don't just ask the butcher for meat, nor do you telephone a general store and ask them to send round some clothes for you to try on. The more specific you can be about your wine likes – and dislikes – the more chance you have of getting something you like and learning a great deal.

Just as no one really enjoys a meal that's virtually thrown at them anyhow, so no one can be expected to enjoy a wine, whether cheap or expensive, that is simply poured out into any old glass in any old way. Most people drink wine for pleasure and the way in which you approach a glass of any wine is quite simple and soon becomes instinctive. Even tasting wine on a more serious scale, such as is done by members of the wine trade, follows the same basic procedure.

What to look for   **The colour** of the wine should be the first consideration, and should give pleasure to the eye. The wine should be clear and bright, with a brilliance about it that can be seen properly only in a clear glass, preferably as thin a glass as possible. If, as you hold the glass by the stem or foot, you tilt it at an angle over something white, such as a napkin or tablecloth, you will see a whole range of tones shading out from the deep 'eye' of colour at the centre of the wine to the point where it meets the glass itself. Only the wine snob or a novice indulges in the act of holding a glass high over the head or waggling it about over a lighted candle.

This shading is rather like the rings in a tree trunk and, in the same way, can indicate the age of the wine. An everyday wine will probably have only two or three tones, but a great wine, whatever age it is, will have many more, its eye being very deep. Very old red wines tend to become lighter in colour and turn rather tawny at the edges; white wines, as they age, darken in colour from pale lemony-gold to almost amber. When you're drinking for pleasure, tones of shading don't matter very much, especially for the beginner, because the important point is that the wine should be bright and beautiful to look at.

As you move the wine around in the glass, does it seem to stick to the glass? In many fine wines, the glycerine in them will make trails down the side of the glass, which is a clear sign of quality.

The smell of the wine should be attractive, giving an impression of health and freshness, and as mentioned before, taste, as wine lovers understand it, is very largely a question of smell. To get the full benefit of a wine's delicious fragrance, swirl it around in the glass (still holding it by the stem or foot), so that the bouquet, as it is called, is released. This is why a wine glass should be bulbous, with the rim curving inwards, to capture the fragrance. It is also the reason why wine should be poured only half-way or, at the most, two-thirds up the glass, because if it is filled to the brim it is virtually impossible to smell the wine – after all, not only is the smell part of the enjoyment of wine, but you have actually paid for it, so why be cheated.

So is the bouquet very pronounced or is it rather reticent, only being evident when you swirl the wine around? Wines which are very definitely scented should never be aggressively so; rather like women who know how to use scent, the fragrance about them should be alluring but never over-powering. Is it 'all of a piece', or does it seem to be made up of several different smells? If there is something about it that you don't like, what is this – mustiness, something chemical or rotten, or a harsh alien tang? At first, these may be difficult to spot but the process will become easier with practice. When you come to taste the wine, see whether or not the smell links up with the taste: does it promise more than the wine ultimately gives, or does it lead up to a very pleasant taste sensation?

It is surprising how few wines actually do smell of grapes! Of course, a very little experience gives you an idea of the different smells associated with the main types of wines, and these may well relate to the grapes that make them, but every single drinker has his or her own idea about smells and what they evoke in the mind. To some people, certain wines conjure up impressions of flowers or fruits; for others, the wines may smell of herbs or stones, even the inside of cigar boxes; some people get an impression of outstanding freshness from a wine, others a sensation of richness.

Taste is very much a personal matter, and you should never try to find out something in a wine simply because somebody has said that, for example, it reminds them of peaches or pears. You'll recall the wine far more if you give it a tag that relates to something you yourself have experienced; perhaps the wine reminds you of a boiled sweet, or has a vague association with lemonade; it may even smell meaty, or remind you of some almost forgotten experience.

You must try to arrive at your own conclusions for yourself. This is why tasting, especially as far as the smell of wines is concerned, is both fascinating and challenging – no one can taste for you, and it is very often hard to try and define something requiring such specialized experience.

Tasting the wine: After you have looked at the wine, swirled it around in the glass and sniffed it, then is the time to taste it and find out if you like it. Take a little wine into your mouth and, if you suck in a scrap of air as well, you will get a much sharper impression of its taste as it gently runs over your gums and the sides of your cheeks.

How does it feel? Is it crisp or velvety in the first impression it makes? Does it make an immediate, almost fierce effect as it comes into your mouth and then die away, or does it start by tasting rather delicate and then build up, so that it seems to bloom in the mouth? Is it hard and acid, or does it pucker up the sides of your mouth (owing to a natural substance called tannin) as if you were eating rhubarb? Or do you get the sensation that it is so strapping, you can almost chew it? But, most important of all, do you or don't you like the taste, and why?

Answering some of these questions will give you a fairly definite idea as to whether or not the wine pleases you, but if it doesn't, then there may be some reason other than the wine itself: you may have drunk or eaten something that has changed your palate, so that even the finest wine would taste less than good, or perhaps you are trying to taste it in a room where there is a lot of cigarette smoke or other smells, which make it impossible to be very critical or even really enjoy a delicate wine.

There is no need to take very long over all of this but, if you can be a little deliberate over your initial tasting of a wine, your first impressions will usually be good guidelines.

Swallowing the wine: Does it go down agreeably, or does it seem sharp and harsh? Do you want to drink more of it? If you do, the wine probably has a special fascination for you which you will be able to associate with this particular wine or others like it in the future. Breathe down your nose into your mouth after you have swallowed the wine: does the aftertaste of the wine seem pleasant and, perhaps, even more fascinating? A great wine should linger in the mouth and charm you by its aftertaste or, as wine lovers often describe it, by the way in which it says 'goodbye' to you.

Making notes Although it is extremely difficult to remember lots of wine names, and harder still to recall the exact impression a wine made on you, even when this was only a day or two ago, you'll find it helpful to make a note of your reaction at the three main stages of tasting: appearance, smell and flavour. Such a record can be invaluable as a guide for both shopping and tasting in the future, and can also be of great interest to you, rather like a dinner party book in which special parties and menus are noted. Even if you do not write down your impressions of the wine, you should at least note the name and signify whether you liked it or not. There's no need to take a long time over your notes – just keep them short and sweet, and to the point.

If you are being really critical and studying wine, proper tasting notes, including the circumstances in which you tried the wines and, if you like, any comments by fellow drinkers, are essential. Should you get the opportunity to taste young wines and can indicate in your notes how they may turn out, this can be of the greatest interest for future reference. However, not even the most experienced and respected member of the wine trade can, without hesitation, pronounce infallibly upon any wine; like people, wines are never wholly predictable and there are often surprises in store even for those who know them best. So don't be disheartened if a wine that you think is going to be delicious when it matures turns out to be a virtual non-starter – or vice versa.

Only experience can give you the confidence to venture your opinions – either written or spoken – but if you never try, you'll never learn.

To spit or not People can be stupidly shy about spitting out wine but, at a professional
to spit . . . tasting, those who don't are conspicuous among the majority who do.

There are several very good reasons for this: if you try to swallow even tiny sips of a dozen or more wines, they will mingle unpleasantly inside you, and you will at best have a headache and possibly indigestion. If you are tasting young wines, they will not be pleasant to drink anyway (although they can be fascinating to smell and take into the mouth), so why do so? And if you are tasting them in a wine region at the property where they are made, they may still be fermenting, so that if you swallow them, they will continue fermenting inside you and upset your stomach. On the other hand, the wines offered for tasting may be ready to drink, but if more than a dozen are set out for you to try, you are unlikely to be able to take more than three or four and retain a clear idea of what they are like if you drink them.

So in these circumstances, don't be self-conscious and do spit out tasting samples. If you only take a little wine into your mouth, you shouldn't find it difficult to eject it neatly into whatever is being used as a spittoon – a bucket, a case of sawdust, or even the floor. Better to be in possession of all your faculties at the end of the tasting, and go on probably to enjoy a meal, than to be fuddled because false modesty made you drink lots of assorted wines.

Incidentally, you'd also be wise not to station yourself too near the spittoon for any length of time, as even those experienced and skilful in the art of spitting out wines – sometimes from quite a distance away – can splash anyone standing too near. It is surprising how people choose the spittoon, rather like the village well, as a focal point for meeting and talking to friends.

The professional tasting

Serious wine tastings are regular events in the life of anyone engaged in the wine trade, but the type of tasting that the wine lover may be invited to will either be of wines that are ready to drink and a merchant wishes to sell, or of young wines which are being tasted, either at the place where they are made, or after they have been moved and are offered for sale. Always bear in mind, however, that a serious tasting is, in fact, an occasion for studying the wines without too much conversation, which can distract tasters; save the gossip and chat for afterwards.

Obviously, a very young wine may not be pleasant to drink; therefore, if you are visiting in vineyard regions, or are invited to taste in someone's cellar, or the office of someone engaged in the wine trade, these may be the sort of wines that will be presented to you. There is nothing difficult about tasting them and much that is interesting, although you should not necessarily expect them to resemble the wines that you drink for enjoyment; what you may be able to do is relate the young wine to the type of wine it will develop into later on.

Wines that are presented for serious tasting when they are going to be sold as ready, or very nearly ready, to drink, will be quite different from young wines, even though some of them may not, in fact, be very old. This naturally depends on the type of wine that is being considered. It is not usual to give a very wide range of wines for tasting at a time, as obviously those who are spending large sums on buying will prefer to concentrate on two, or possibly three, main styles. It would be confusing to have, say, German and French wines from several regions all in the same tasting. There may, with tastings of wines that are ready to drink be some variation in their age, whereas when young wines are tasted, they are generally all of the same age.

The tasting procedure and the attitude of mind of the taster can be trained and adapted to a routine, so that something is learned from each tasting experience. It is obviously more enjoyable to be doing something active at a tasting than simply standing around and waiting for someone to make a pronouncement or for lunch to be served! And people who are possibly going to spend large sums of money on buying the wines need their attention solely on what is in the glass in front of them and should not talk too much.

Personal wine tastings

If you have become seriously interested in wine, quite likely you and your friends may wish to arrange study session tastings for yourself. Ideally, try to do this with the help and advice of someone more experienced, preferably a member of the wine trade, because, as with learning any subject, it helps to have guidance at the beginning so that you do not waste time and money. But personal tastings of this kind are usually quite informal, with people contributing the wines and then discussing them, having previously found out as much as they can about their own contributions.

Sometimes people like to compare the vintages of one great estate, at other times a selection of wines from a particular vintage may be under discussion, or examples of wines made from the same grape, but coming from different regions and different countries. It is a good idea to restrict the number of wines to about half a dozen so that people don't take too long about this sort of study session tasting, and it is up to you whether you offer any refreshment or just drink up the wines after you have studied them.

With all tasting, however, it is sense to follow certain rules: do not try to taste too many wines at a time, as it is a tiring business. Have a drink or wash your mouth out with water, if you wish, but otherwise do not eat or drink anything in the middle of the tasting, unless you take a piece of biscuit or dry bread (members of the wine trade pertinently say, 'We buy on apples, sell on cheese', and this is why they will seldom taste anything alkaline, such as cheese, during a tasting, simply because it makes all the wines taste too good!) No one with any consideration for others would wear scent or use anything on themselves or their clothes with a strong smell, which might distract the tasters; women are often criticized for this kind of thing, but often men, with their aftershave, boot polish, pipes in pockets, and hair preparations, can be just as great offenders.

As regards smoking, of course, no one with any manners would smoke in a tasting, although many people are glad of the opportunity to do so afterwards. So, if you are in a professional tasting room, where the atmosphere is kept as clean and unpolluted as possible, it is only sense to ask if you may light a cigarette after the tasting is finished.

Chapter 5 *Shopping for Wine*

There are numerous places where you can buy good wine, and the wise shopper will know how to make the best use of each retail outlet. Britain is particularly fortunate, because nowhere else in the world is there quite such a wide range of wines to choose from, available from so many different types of retailer, any one of which should be delighted to sell to all kinds of customer. So there is no need to be timid about going in to one of the more historic-looking wine merchant's, nor need you apologize if you give your dinner guests a supermarket wine recently on offer as a special bargain. The sensible thing is to know which of the various outlets is likely to be most helpful to you, the buyer.

The wine merchant Although everyone in the wine trade offering wine for sale to the public would describe him (or her) self as a wine merchant, the customer generally thinks of a wine merchant in terms of an establishment specializing in wines and spirits and nothing else. This merchant may be an independent concern – and some of these are historic family businesses, with long-established traditions. The merchant may also be, as it were, the showcase of a very large multiple retail organization, perhaps one owned by a large concern, such as a brewery, but having one retail outlet of particular and specialized importance. But the important thing to bear in mind about going to a merchant of this kind is that there should be people behind the counter, with some specialized knowledge of the wines which they handle, so that they can advise the customer not only on *what* to buy for some immediate occasion, but also *how* money can be wisely spent as a saving in the future.

If you live near a wine merchant of this kind, do not hesitate to become a customer, even for the most humble wines. Remember, it is on the cheapest wines on the list that the merchant's reputation is built! Of course, it isn't sensible to go in late in the evening or in the pre-Christmas rush and expect to have a lengthy conversation with an authority about the particular bottle you are hoping to buy; but becoming a regular customer, even by means of the most modest purchases, can have many advantages. You can study his

PLATE 4: *A familiar landmark on the Moselle skyline is Landshut Castle, which perches high on a hill overlooking the village of Bernkastel, home of some of the greatest Moselle wines.*

PLATES 5, 6 and 7: *Wine is made from an amazing number of different grapes, but only a few of them make the great wines. Here are three of them: the white Chardonnay (left) makes Champagne as well as white Burgundy and Chablis in particular; the Pinot noir (centre) makes red Burgundy and Champagne; and the Palomino (right) is the principal grape grown in Spain for sherry.*

wine list and note what savings can be made; you can specify exactly the occasion for which you are buying wine, the kind of food you are going to serve, as well as the sort of money you can afford to pay without any hesitation. All these points are of interest to the man behind the counter, who will take a personal pride in giving you a wine, even a modest half-bottle, which may, if his judgement is right, bring you back for more and so encourage you to become a regular customer.

The merchant will also be able to listen to any complaints or criticisms you may have; any merchant should replace a bottle that is out of condition, but it takes a specialist to understand why you didn't like a wine and to choose something else for you. And, if you are on a merchant's mailing list, he'll let you know about any sales, perhaps of remnants or bin ends, which should be of interest. Some merchants also hold tastings for regular customers, at which you can sample a number of wines, and this is the kind of merchant to ask for advice if you are going abroad and would like to have an introduction in one of the classic wine regions to see a particular vineyard or cellar.

It isn't necessary to have only one wine merchant, however eminent. No single firm could ever know all and stock everything, even at the request of a multi-millionaire! But a good wine merchant can give very helpful service. Most retailers loan out glasses (the only charges made are usually for breakages), supply wines on a sale or return basis (which means the merchant will take back unopened bottles and not charge you), and possibly loan such accessories as punch bowls and ladles for a special party. Sometimes they can advise on suitable mixed drinks, and help if you are arranging some function by way of a wine tasting. And there is absolutely no reason for a woman to be shy about shopping for wine at the most eminent wine merchants.

Retail chains and multiples Many large firms, such as Stowell's and Thresher's, Peter Dominic, Victoria Wine and similar organizations, have retail shops that literally cover the country. These concerns usually have a very long list, although they obviously cannot stock every single one of the very finest wines at all the branches, and, therefore, may need a little notice for the more obscure wines. But most of these firms can offer excellent service as regards stock and deliveries, and they will also have someone in charge who, thanks to the excellent education programmes now run by most of the large concerns, will have some specialized knowledge of wines and spirits in general.

Beers, soft drinks and similar additions to the wine scene can also be bought from them and very often the party and catering services provided by such retailers are of great help to host and hostesses.

Sometimes people think that there is something vaguely second-rate about buying wine from a multiple and feel they have to apologize for their dinner-party drinks. How wrong they are, because it is precisely the size of the firm behind the multiples that enables a number of the wines exclusive to them to be sold at reasonable prices, and as far as some of the very largest firms are concerned, they can actually dictate the policy of some of the wine regions and thereby maintain standards of quality. Such retailers will have their own special lines, as well as possibly their own brands of spirits, which can also be offered at bargain prices because they do not have to bear the costs of national advertising. The men behind the wine-buying of such businesses are highly knowledgeable and experienced, and in trying to cater for a huge range of customers they have a very good idea of what will please and bring people back for more.

At the same time, it would be unreasonable to assume that the busy manager of a small multiple doing heavy business in everyday drinks is able to spare much time for detailed discussion about a particular wine problem, nor can it be assumed that he will always have the specific knowledge to solve such a problem. The good manager should be able to find out – but again, he is only human. However, multiple chains often have tastings for their customers, also special promotions, so that customers can try out a range of wines newly introduced, and no one should be deterred from asking the opinion of the salesman as to what may please when planning a party.

The off-licence The use of the term 'off-licence' has very little significance today, because obviously wherever wine is bought for consumption off the premises, it is an 'off-licence'! But the wine department of a pub that sells bottles to take away has become associated with this term, which is how it is used here.

With public houses or bars owned by any of the large concerns, such as breweries or wine chains, the wines available for buying will obviously be those which are the firm's staple lines. As mentioned above, these wines can be good value, if only because big firms have to stay in business by giving the customers what they want at prices they can afford to pay. For reasons of space, a very wide range of wines and spirits will obviously not be available here, although the proprietary brands of the group owning the concern will naturally be featured, together with other best-selling lines, as well as the everyday, staple wines and spirits. If you run out of wine or have unexpected guests, then the off-licence can be a reliable source of supply, although, ideally, it should not be the only one.

The wine department of a big store The wine buyer of any of the big stores is an important and experienced person, probably with a vast stock at his disposal. He should have a very good idea of the requirements of his customers, particularly for medium- and low-priced wines, and will also carry special lines for special occasions.

But, of course, he needs to turn his stock over fairly rapidly and, therefore, will usually concentrate on what has been established as a popular type of wine. Assistants in such a department should also have gained knowledge by working with the buyer.

The special lines and occasional bargains offered by the wine department of stores are always worth looking at, and the associated services offered, such as parking facilities and occasions when the store's catering department can also be called in, are well worth investigating.

The licenced grocer   Sometimes this kind of establishment will be a big and rather smart provisions store, while others are more of a general shop in the High Street. Depending on the range of stock carried, it can be a valuable source of supply for wines and spirits, with special offers and bargains appearing, and, of course, adjuncts to entertaining, such as nuts and crisps, soft drinks, and food, such as cheese, usually being available too. It would be unfair to expect the manager of this kind of retail outlet to have a detailed knowledge of fine wines (although very often he may have), but his stock should be reliable and reasonably comprehensive.

The super-market wine department   If the supermarket is entirely self-service, then the customer must obviously know a little about wine to choose a suitable bottle from the rack. Sometimes supermarkets do have an assistant standing by to give advice to customers. But, although good wines may be stocked by supermarkets, it would obviously be unreasonable to expect to find vast ranges of fine wines kept under the glare of the artificial light and in the hurly-burly of such a store.

The supermarket is the place to shop for inexpensive everyday wine, and the house brands and special offers of such places are always likely to be of interest and can be of great value. The buyers for the supermarkets, again, are people who would not risk their firms' capital on items unlikely to appeal to the customer and their house brands of wines and spirits can be definite bargains.

Wine auctions   Because wine is a subject of great interest to people today, the enormous prices some of the great wines in the world fetch at the big auctions in London and elsewhere tend to make news. But this does not mean that wine auctions are either wholly concerned with top price wines or, in fact, that they invariably offer great bargains. As with any other commodity sold by auction, prospective buyers need to know something about the subject before they bid, and, as most lots are in multiples of dozens, you must be very sure indeed, of what you are doing before bidding for several dozen bottles. Sometimes, too, the excitement of the sale causes bidders to force the price of a quite ordinary wine way above what it is currently quoted on the lists of other merchants.

If you particularly want to buy certain wines offered by the great wine departments of auctioneers such as Christie, Manson & Woods, and Sotheby's in London, then ideally it is worth taking the advice of your wine merchant first, both as to the kind of price that may be expected from certain lots, and also to consider whether you really want as much wine as you are likely to have to buy. A wine merchant will usually bid for you if you cannot attend the sale yourself, and sometimes a group of friends can combine to buy wine in this way. As with all sales, it is important to know what you are doing, to set a limit on how much you are prepared to spend, and to take into account any delivery charges which may subsequently have to be met when the wine is delivered.

Wine clubs Wine clubs became very popular before the abolition of retail price maintenance, and essentially they provide a means of buying in bulk at wholesale prices. Although buying through a wine club enables the prospective purchaser to choose from the list at leisure, at home, before simply sending off the order, it can have some disadvantages. After all, any wine merchant will accept a written order drawn from a list in just the same way – and he can offer other services as well.

If you belong to a trade or professional organization, with its own wine club, it is worth checking on the following points before you make substantial purchases:

1 Is there an entrance fee, and what sort of subscription is required?

2 Must you buy unmixed cases (a case equals a dozen bottles) of wines or spirits, or can these be in mixed dozens? (Sometimes big price savings are offered on spirits, but the saving on wines is not so much.)

3 Can you buy known brands of wines and spirits, or are you restricted to club purchases? A club may have excellent wines and spirits bottled under its own label, but if you only like to drink a particular well-known brand, you may feel that this is a disadvantage. And if only club brands are available, can you taste these at any time before you buy?

4 Must you pay carriage on your purchases or are they carriage paid? If you have to pay delivery charges and it is difficult for you to receive deliveries of wines, then you may be effecting little or no saving.

5 Is the wine club associated with one wine firm or organization – and if so, which one? A reputable concern can offer a wide range of reputable wines and spirits, but unknown brands and names, from an obscure source of supply can be doubtful bargains. When you investigate this, you should also find out who actually is the wine buyer – is it done by a committee, representative of the club's members, or is there

an unknown person in charge of the buying or a celebrity, who may be an enthusiastic drinker but whose wine knowledge is negligible? All these things should be easily found out in any reputable wine club.

6 Is the selection of wines on the club list very limited? If so, then you are restricting yourself to only a few lines which you might buy as inexpensively elsewhere – and have more fun exploring other ranges! Of course, if you simply want any old wine at a low price, then this probably doesn't matter, but one assumes that you are, or hope to be, a discriminating drinker.

7 Is the minimum order a dozen bottles; if so, have you adequate storage space for this? Remember, you tend to drink what you have in your home, so if you find that your consumption rises sharply simply because you have several cases of wine delivered at regular intervals, then you are not really effecting a saving by buying in this way. And how convenient is it to store quantities of wine anyway?

8 Does the club have any associated activities, such as regular tastings, study sessions, and perhaps visits to wine regions? Some clubs organize functions for members, and this can be an admirable and very pleasant way of learning about wine, but if membership of a wine club merely gives you bulk-buying facilities, then you will do well to reflect that you can buy wine in bulk at most other outlets.

Wine offers in newspapers and magazines
From time to time special wine selections are offered through newspapers and magazines and can represent real value for the purchaser. Usually, the selection has been made in conjunction with one particular firm, and whoever has done the selecting may write a few notes on the wines offered. Buying wine in this way is rather like following the recommendations of a critic as regards a play or film – you are allying yourself with one particular individual. Usually, wines offered for sale in this way cannot be returned if you do not like them, but it is fair to say that this comparatively new way of offering wine to the public has proved highly successful and many wine merchants have found regular and knowledgeable customers as a result of an initial purchase made through such a special offer.

Wines offered in advertisements are like any other commodity so offered – they can be great bargains, but phrases such as '50p. off normal price' or 'unrepeatable bargain', or a string of flowery adjectives describing an unknown wine may mean very little. The special offers of a reputable wine firm will always be of interest, and sometimes case lots of such wines can be offered because the merchant simply wishes to clear the cellars of them. Wines purchased in this way can always be queried with the merchant if you think there is something genuinely wrong with them. Bin ends, or small quantities of wines which are no longer worth listing but which are in perfect condition, are stock which is often shifted in this way. But, of course, if you are buying entirely by mail order, you should cost in the postage and packing for any bottles you may have to return, including correspondence or telephone calls on which you have to spend time and money.

Cut-price wine shops Comparatively recently there has been an enormous amount of business done by firms offering wines and spirits at wholesale prices or sometimes even lower. These firms have done a great service to wine by encouraging people to buy wine regularly and fairly casually, but there are several things to take into consideration before deciding, as many people do, that this is the one and only way to buy wine.

Very often such stock offered at low prices is perfectly genuine, and may come as a result of purchasing bankrupt stock elsewhere or from reserves that have been put on the market or that other merchants wish to dispose of. But no one, very often not even the salesman handling the goods, can be sure exactly where they come from and whether or not they are in first-rate condition; nor, however obliging the sales staff, can they always replace a bottle which is totally out of condition.

Of course, all transactions in shops of this kind are on a cash and carry basis, which can also be a means of saving money in the most eminent wine merchants as well as in the cut-price concerns. You cannot expect staff, in a shop where they are primarily concerned with a quick turnover of stock, to have detailed information about wine, and it would be unreasonable to do so. Nor can you expect to have a wine list with descriptive matter or information, and, of course, delivery and similar allied services are likely to be either cut down or even abolished.

The accessibility of cut-price wine shops is a big factor in their favour, because parking is becoming increasingly difficult in many areas where wine merchants have their establishments. But if you buy a quantity of wine on a cash and carry basis, are you yourself able to carry it to your car, or do you have to tip whoever is helping you – which of course, adds to the overall cost? Do you know enough about wine to buy something in this way, and be pretty sure that you are getting a bargain and not just a good-looking label? Wine that has been in shop windows, exposed to the sun, in flooded or damaged warehouses, left in transit for too long, or was not bottled when it should have been, can be far from at its best and this is the risk that the customer takes when buying below normal shop prices. It is up to him to gamble on getting a bargain or spoiling a dinner party.

Buying direct from a producer Sometimes people get the idea that they will effect great savings if they import wine, in cask, direct from a producer in a wine region. Although this can be done satisfactorily, there are numerous disadvantages, and perhaps it is significant that people in the wine trade (who have all the facilities to hand) don't actually do this.

First of all, can you *really* judge a young wine? It may taste very different in cask, where it is made, from when it has been bottled for some time. Then, if it is really as good as you may believe, why hasn't some local restaurant, wine dealer or, even, international shipper bought it anyway – they're always looking for bargains and they have the advantage over the layman.

If you are definite about buying it, are you prepared to cope with the expense of getting it to you, with the various forms and insurances, the duty, the handling charges, the delivery itself and, if necessary, dealing with any problems if something goes wrong en route? As even the big firms in the trade know, wines can get lost, delayed, damaged or held beyond the time when they should be bottled; and if they arrive in imperfect condition, do you have facilities to get these set right?

Even then, your troubles are not over. Can you and your friends cope with the bottling? Have you the necessary equipment and can you spare the time? Wine can't be left hanging about until you feel in the mood to bottle it and, as there are 48 gallons in a cask, this is quite a job; it must be completed in a single operation or else the wine may be spoiled. And, as there is quite a large quantity in a cask – even in a quarter cask – do you really *want* all that wine, even if it is cheap? Wouldn't it be more enjoyable to have a change now and again, especially if the wine doesn't turn out so marvellous?

Should you be set on importing your own choice of wine, you would be well advised to ask a merchant with experience in handling wine, to do it for you. His knowledge will be a safeguard and a saving of your time and money. He may also, if you wish, arrange to import any bottled wine for you, also sparing you the complications of the various formalities. He will also know exactly what to do if something goes wrong.

So, unless you are a chemist, have worked in the wine trade or are able to call on expert assistance, always eschew buying and handling wine direct from a grower yourself. Buy the odd case, as a souvenir of a holiday but, even then you may find that it simply doesn't give you the same enjoyment, once you get it home, as some of your wine merchant's listed items. Ask him, anyway, before you take what can be very expensive action.

Saving money when buying wine There are many ways of effecting quite considerable savings when you are buying both wines and spirits, whether you are making your purchases from a traditional wine merchant with imposing premises, or from a nearby supermarket or off-licence. It is sensible shopping to be aware of these potential ways to cut corners and you need have no hesitation about asking for discounts to which you are fully entitled.

Buying by the case
First of all, buying wines and spirits by the dozen should entitle you to a 'case' discount, and if you are contemplating buying in dozens, then ideally you should get a quotation from more than one source of supply, so as to see how much you may save. Sometimes you can get this discount on cases of mixed wines and spirits, or only on one or the other; sometimes the wine must be all of one kind, the spirits likewise.

Nevertheless, it pays to find out.

Cash payment
If you pay cash, then very often you will get a cash discount, sometimes even on purchases of a single bottle. This, in fact, is the whole basis of the cash and carry principle. But don't forget to cost into this what you have to pay for travelling to and from the source of supply, and how much *this* will cost you in terms of transport and time.

Ordering by post
If you put an order through the post for wine, you may get a discount for cash with order, just as you do with cash and carry. Or there may be special terms for payment within 30 days. When buying by post, you must check whether postage or delivery is charged – it is uneconomical for many firms to send quantities of less than a dozen bottles, but sometimes this may be done for goodwill – an important point to consider if you send wine as a present. Postage can be costly these days, and packing is certainly expensive; with deliveries you may also have to tip the delivery man, unless you can hump the case of wine yourself when he unloads it.

Some merchants include a reply-paid card for orders in their lists. But if you can telephone your order, are the firm involving you only in the expense of a local call? If you have a complaint, can you, without much time, money or trouble, get through to someone who will put it right, or do you have to write a letter and pay for the return of any damaged goods?

Always read the small print at the back or front of the lists of most wine merchants. If you study the terms of sale, you may find that you can buy, even from the most imposing-looking merchant, as advantageously as from a cash and carry or cut-price firm. But you must take the trouble to find out – otherwise, your experience may be won more expensively than you bargained for!

Understanding the bottle label
Another important aspect of buying wine is understanding what information is given on bottle labels. The range of wines and spirits available in the United Kingdom is so enormous that no hard and fast definition of what should be found on labels can be made, because each producing country will have its own legislation governing this. Buyers of wine are sometimes surprised to know that there are such strict controls on labelling but, even if the regulations are complied with, there are still enormous variations

possible in label design; it is good marketing to have an easily recognizable label of a distinctive type, which complies with the generally-accepted notion of good taste.

But it is rather sad that the public will 'buy on the label' to such a marked extent that they will think that an elaborately-labelled bottle (probably also widely promoted by advertising in publications and on television) contains a wine superior to that coming from a bottle rather simply and traditionally labelled. Some firms and the owners of some great wine estates change their labels frequently, others have always kept them the same, and this is obviously a matter of an establishment's policy; however, it does tend to be true that the appeal of a stridently-labelled bottle, of many colours and possibly with gold and silver added, bearing a number of different lettering styles and obviously invented *historic* pictures or legends, will be trying to make up for the uncertain quality of its contents.

The greatest wines and spirits, even if their labels are elaborate, are invariably in good taste, although sometimes this may seem outmoded according to whatever is currently in vogue in the world of advertising. The real quality product seldom needs to scream out about itself and, when a new label is designed, for all but the everyday and obviously 'fun' wines, the simpler it is, the better. Over-elaborate labels are rather like over-dressed, bejewelled women – too much of a good thing – and a very elaborate presentation, other than special gift packs, may be expenditure diverted to this sort of packaging that should rightly be spent on the quality of the drink.

Types of label As well as the main label on the wine bottle, there may be others.

The neck label goes round the lower part of the neck or on the shoulder of the bottle, and sometimes gives either the vintage date of a wine or the name of the shipper.

The back label goes opposite the main label and sometimes provides background information about the particular wine.

The strip label can go under the main label, almost at the bottom of the bottle, and is sometimes used by the merchant or the shipper for an estate-bottled wine.

Neck tag: Occasionally a bottle is further adorned with a tag around its neck, which also gives background information about the firm producing it and suggestions as to how the wine is to be served.

Protection of names Rules governing the statements made on all these labels are in operation, so that it is not possible, for example, to use a name or a phrase that may give a false impression of the wine. A red Bordeaux cannot be called *château*, *domaine* or *clos* something, unless it actually does come from a single property of that name; if it is simply a blend of wines from various regions and, say, there is no such estate as Château Zaza, then this name cannot be used in conjunction with the word 'château' on the label.

Many great estates have different labels for their wines that are bottled at the property and those that are bottled by the shipper, and should the label of the estate be used for wines bottled away from the property, then the information about where the bottling took place will be given either on the bottom of the label or on a strip label.

As mentioned before, certain wine names are specially protected: like Champagne, which in France, the U.K. and the other E.E.C. countries, can only be used for the wine from the Champagne region in France; this regulation does not, however, apply to Spain, the U.S.A. and many other countries, so that sparkling wines produced by all three can be sold as Champagne without prosecution. In Britain, port can come only from Portugal and sherry from the sherry region of Spain; if any wine made in a sherry-style in any other country comes into the U.K., the law requires that its country of origin shall appear on the label before the word 'sherry', if this is used at all, in the same lettering style and size. It cannot simply be called sherry. It must be called, for example, Cyprus sherry, South African sherry, or British sherry.

Spirits are similarly protected and most of the world-famous wine and spirit firms have museums or collections of the imitations of their product; some are very obvious frauds, others are very skilful. There is the tale of the Japanese whisky which, according to the label, was 'Prepared at Buckingham Palace under the personal supervision of His Majesty'!

Information on the label

When shopping for wines and spirits, do not be intimidated by what seems to be a complicated label. A little consideration and, as it were, taking it to pieces, will show you that a lot of information is given to help you get an idea of what the wine is like without tasting it, and to provide some point of reference for you should there be any query or complaint after you have tried it.

For example, on the label of every bottle of Champagne you will see some small numbers at the bottom, which are the means whereby this particular wine is identified, even if it is sold under a name that is otherwise wholly unknown except to the one merchant who has had it bottled. You can follow up this reference, if necessary, by contacting the body in Champagne who supervises the quality of the wine – the C.I.V.C. (Comité Interprofessionel du Vin de Champagne). Of course, this is an extreme example, but a firm putting out a quality product at any price level will be proud of this and not make it difficult for any customer to get in touch with them should there be a problem about the wine.

A label is there primarily to identify the wine and inform the customer.

Regulations are increasingly providing more information, and the various wine and spirit trade associations are becoming more and more concerned to protect the good name of their members, so that the label to beware of is the one that either gives inadequate information or a great deal of what your own commonsense tells you is matter of a rather dubious nature. Once again, shopping for wine is like shopping for anything else and you soon develop some notion as to what is likely to be good by looking at the package, thereby gaining some impression of the style of the source of the bottle.

British labelling British law affecting wine labelling is primarily dictated by the Trades Descriptions Act of 1968. It is possible that, one day – and at least within the E.E.C. – one set of international regulations will apply to all wines and spirits, protecting both consumer and producer against abuses, but at the present time British law requires only that labels must include:

1 'An appropriate designation', which indicates the style of the contents of the bottle, such as red wine, vodka, or, more specifically, the name of a particular wine-producing estate or spirit distillery.

2 The country of origin. This is why many labels carry the phrase, 'Produce of France', although the actual name of the contents of the bottle may also include the origin of the liquid, such as 'Australian Hock', or 'London Gin'.

3 The name and address of the bottler or labeller or the firm for which the drink was bottled.

4 The strength of spirit in degrees Sikes for spirits and liqueurs and what is described as 'processed wines', such as vermouth. If the bottle contains more than 3 fl. oz spirits and liqueurs, the fluid content must also be given, but, of course, a miniature holds less than this.

If the fluid content is specified on the label, then the contents must be precisely that. Of course, this can sometimes present problems if a customer is ignorant of the fact that, particularly with fine wines which have been kept for some time, the ullage or space of air between the top of the wine and the bottom of the cork has increased. It is unlikely, however, that anyone knowing enough about wines in this category would bring an action against the wine merchant, and in any case the difficulty of being precise about the exact contents of a bottle, with variations in length of corks, ullage, and the actual thickness of the glass, is something which is perennially under discussion. However, as far as spirits are concerned, because they do not evaporate in the bottle, the fluid contents of what the bottle should contain must be given on the label.

Labelling laws in other countries As has already been indicated, labelling laws vary, but the following laws relate particularly to the wines of France, Italy and Germany, and have recently come increasingly into force.

France

About 15 per cent of the wines made in France possess an *Appellation d'Origine Contrôlée* (usually abbreviated to *Appellation Contrôlée*, A.O.C., or A.C.), which literally means Restricted Name of Origin. Many people are under the impression that this is an automatic guarantee of quality, but only the care and conscientiousness of the producer, the shipper and the merchant can guarantee any such thing directly.

What the laws of *Appellation* do is to define, for each one of the major or fine wine regions of France, the following: where the vines are grown; the grape varieties; the way the vines are cultivated, how many can be planted and the yield from particular areas; the amount of wine that can be made, its alcoholic strength, and the exact name that can be used for the wine.

Grades of appellation As far as this last point is concerned, there are *appellations* or names going up in stages, as it were, so that among the great red wines of Bordeaux, you start with the straightforward A.O.C. **Bordeaux**, then **Bordeaux Supérieure**, then, possibly, one of the districts, such as **Médoc, St. Emilion,** or **Graves**. At this stage, the *appellations* get more complicated. In the Médoc, for example, a number of the communes or parishes have their own *appellations*, so that a fine wine such as Château Palmer, will be labelled *Appellation Margaux Contrôlée*. The fact that Margaux is in the Médoc, that the wine is a very superior type of Bordeaux Supérieure, and that the region is Bordeaux need not be stated, because the *appellation* **Margaux** is superior to all these. Similarly in Burgundy each particular vineyard district will have its own *appellation*, although **Bourgogne** is the lowest form of Burgundy A.O.C.

The way the *appellations* fit inside each other in this way is not a matter to trouble anyone buying wine – they can always be looked up in a reference book. It does mean, however, that a very fine wine should have a *particular* rather than a *general* A.O.C., and by implication the wine is likely to be good, although it cannot be guaranteed to be so. The possession of an *appellation* is rather like having a pedigree or a good education – by implication, the individual possessing either or both should be good, but of course, nothing can guarantee that they will be so!

There is a lower *appellation*, known as *Vins Délimités de Qualité Supérieure* (V.D.Q.S. for short), for minor wines; these are not quite as strictly controlled as the A.O.C.'s but are nevertheless subject to regulations as regards where and how they are made. They are becoming increasingly important to

VOLNAY-CAILLERETS

APPELLATION VOLNAY CONTRÔLÉE

TRADE MARK

Récolte des
DOMAINES JABOULET-VERCHERRE

Négociant à Beaune, Côte d'Or

1

PRODUCE OF FRANCE

JLP LEBÈGUE ET CIE À BEAUNE CÔTE D'OR

MEURSAULT
BLAGNY

Appellation Contrôlée

MIS EN BOUTEILLES EN FRANCE

J L P Lebègue

BATTLEBRIDGE HOUSE TOOLEY ST. LONDON SE1

SHIPPERS OF FINE WINES

2

3

4

5

6

FRENCH TABLE WINES (1): **1** The Caillerets vineyards are among the top growths in the commune of Volnay in the Côte de Beaune. The word '*Récolte*' means 'harvest', indicating that the wine came from the Domaines or property of Jaboulet-Vercherre, and the word '*Negociant*' denotes the proprietor is also the shipper of the wine. **2** A white Côte d'Or Burgundy from the Blagny vineyards in the commune of Meursault. It is bottled in France (*mis en bouteilles en France*) by the shippers. **3** An estate-bottled wine (*mis en bouteilles au château*) from the oldest known vineyard in Châteauneuf-du-Pape. **4** An outstanding Château wine from the Médoc commune of Pauillac, bottled by the Bordeaux shippers. **5** A Château wine, bottled by the shipper, from one of the Bordeaux's lesser red wine districts, Premières Côtes de Blaye. **6** A famous sweet white Bordeaux from Château Climens in the Barsac district.

FRENCH TABLE WINES (2): **1** An estate-bottled (*mise en bouteille à la propriété*) Gewürztraminer from Alsace. **2** A Château-bottled wine, with a V.D.Q.S. appellation, from one of France's lesser wine districts, Coteaux d'Aix en Provence. **3** A regional V.D.Q.S. red wine from the minor district Côtes de Ventoux. **4** A popular branded Anjou Rosé, bottled by the shipper, from the Loire valley. **5** A single grape wine from the Loire valley. **6** This single grape wine from Bordeaux shows how the phrase '*Blanc de Blancs*' can be used for a wine other than Champagne.

all wine drinkers, now that the prices of the finest A.O.C. wines have risen so high. There are also some lesser categories of wines by virtue of their area and production, and, at the very bottom of the scale, there are good blended wines, which probably will simply be entitled 'Produce of France'.

French spirits and some apéritifs are also subject to the rules of *Appellation Contrôlée*, and it may be of interest to know that so are certain foodstuffs, including the famous Bresse chickens! The great exception to the A.O.C. rules is Champagne, which the French controlling body for wines and spirits permits simply to use the phrase *Vin de Champagne* on the labels. Another point worth remembering is that it is the local syndicates of wine growers who determine the specific regulations governing the awarding of the A.O.C. in their different areas, and that these regulations are not all the same through-out the whole of France.

Italy

In 1963 a law was passed in Italy affecting Italian-bottled wines only. This is the system known as *Denominazione di Origine Controllata* (abbreviated to D.O.C.). This also determines the area where certain wines may be produced, the way the vineyard is arranged, the grapes and blends of grapes and methods of cultivation used, the yield of the vineyard, the method of vinification and length of time for maturing the wines, and which wines of different vintages can be blended. The types of bottles and labels, the names of wines and firms are also controlled; no high-sounding but spurious names implying their owners belong to some wine dynasty are permitted, and the penalties for infringement of any of these regulations can result in an offending establishment being both fined per offending litre of wine and closed for a year.

Many people are under the impression that D.O.C. is the same as the French A.O.C., but it does not really work in the same way, being directly under the Ministry of Agriculture in Rome, and not affected so much by the local syndicates. Also, considerable time has been taken over the granting of the D.O.C. to many well-known wines, sometimes simply because of the lack of agreement on certain methods of viticulture and vinification, how-ever traditional, and also because, in many historic vineyards, the exact area is difficult to determine. A wine possessing the D.O.C. clearly states this on the label, and this, which has been granted to only 149 wines at the time of writing, also implies quality, although naturally it cannot guarantee it. There is a superior classification, *Denominazione di Origine Controllata e Guarantita*, but to date, this has not been awarded to any wine.

The buyer of Italian wines must, therefore, depend a great deal on the name, both of the wine and the importer, should the wine be bottled *outside* Italy, and although there is naturally very great pride on the part of those

1

2

3

4

5

6

ITALIAN TABLE WINE LABELS: **1** A quality Valpolicella, an appealing red wine from the Veneto region of Italy. **2** A branded wine from the Veneto sold in a distinctively-shaped 2 litre bottle. **3** Orvieto, bottled in the traditional wicker-bound flask like Chianti, is the outstanding white wine from Umbria in Central Italy. **4** This Barbera comes specifically from the Asti district in Piedmont; the word 'Superiore' denotes the wine is of higher quality than plain Barbera. **5** Barolo, the great red wine of Piedmont, takes its name from a village. The word 'Classico' denotes that the wine comes from the best vineyards in the district. **6** Chianti, from Tuscany, is certainly the best-known Italian red wine. The words '*Vino infiascato nella zona di produzione*' mean that the wine was bottled in the traditional wicker-bound flask in the area of origin.

producers of D.O.C. wines, many of those wines which have applied and are still being considered for D.O.C. should not be overlooked, until the whole of Italy has had time to submit its wines for this carefully awarded classification.

Germany

The reason why German wine labels seem difficult to understand is because they carry lots of information and also because the old Gothic script used by many firms makes it difficult for the person who does not speak German to decipher the long names. It is only fair to comment that many English names present exactly the same type of difficulties to non-English speaking people!

Recently the Germans attempted to protect and control further the quality of their wines by means of a new German wine law, taking effect from the 1971 vintage, but there have been enormous difficulties in applying this exactly, modifications are still being made and, of course, many of the finer wines, labelled before the 1971 vintage, are still on sale. One cynic among the German wine growers observed that anyone world famous for making the finest of German wines who just went on making them would go to prison, whereas anyone attempting to conform to all the requirements of the new wine law would go into an asylum!

Types of wine As far as the customer is concerned, the basic divisions of wines are as follows (in German, the umlaut '¨' symbol above a letter represents the sound of that letter and, when it is not possible to print this, an additional 'e' can be used instead; this makes it easier to pronounce, so therefore the 'e' spelling is used here):

Deutscher Tafelwein, meaning German table wine, is not allowed to use a vineyard name and need not come from any specific vineyard or be made from any particular grape.

Qualitaetswein bestimmter Anbaugebiete (abbreviated to **QbA**) is a wine of quality from a specific area of production and from specified grapes, which must attain a certain alcoholic strength in the must before any sweetening is added.

Qualitaetswein mit Praedikat is a quality wine with detailed qualifications. This last category of wine has to attain a higher must strength, the grapes and the area from which it comes are strictly defined, and the wines cannot be sweetened in any way, having to be purely dependent on the natural grape sugar. As many German vineyards are divided up into small plots (somewhat like Burgundy vineyards), with many growers making their wines by the single cask and keeping these apart from others made in the same vineyard, wines in the Qualitaetswein categories will bear a particular number on the label, to distinguish one individual wine from another from the same vineyard.

Bottling terms   Various terms have been used in the past for wines bottled by the producer, such as *Originalabfuellung* but, in general, the words *Erzeuger-Abfuellung* or *Aus eigenem Lesegut* (meaning from own vineyard) now signify 'Estate-bottled' for both categories of Qualitaetswein. However, a wine bottled elsewhere than on the estate, by a shipper, for example, may be described by the phrase *Aus dem Lesegut des Winzers* (meaning from the producer's own cellars).

The styles of   The following descriptions are used in addition to the other names on the
German Wine   label to denote either the degree of quality of the wine or the way in which it has been made. It is important to have these terms clear in one's mind, because each type of wine is so very different, and not all-purpose by any means.

Cabinet: This term might be best translated by 'Special Reserve' as the wine is carefully tested and tasted before being approved.

Spaetlese (pronounce the first syllable to rhyme with 'late', the second two to rhyme with 'mazer'): This term means that the grapes have been gathered late, when they will have become very ripe, and so endow the wine, when this is made, with a more intense, definite flavour.

Auslese (pronounce the first syllable to rhyme with 'mouse'): This term means that when the grapes have been gathered they have been picked over, so that only the finest and ripest are used to make the wine, which is kept separately. Auslese wines are always very fine and tend to possess a beautiful ripe, intensely fruity flavour, bordering on sweetness, but never being cloying.

Beerenauslese (pronounce the first two syllables just as you think they read): This term means that the actual grapes used to make this type of wine are selected from the bunches one by one, and the wine is again kept apart. These wines have a wonderful fragrance – one might say they 'bloom' in the glass – and they should be slowly sipped, never gulped. Apart from anything else, they are not really wines for serving with food, but come into the category of drinks to enjoy quite alone, or perhaps with luscious fruits like peaches and nectarines, and in an atmosphere clear of tobacco smoke and other smells. They are some of the greatest white wines of the world.

Trockenbeerenauslese (the first syllable rhymes with 'frock'): This term means that the grapes from which these wines are made have been left on the vines longer than all the others, and the action of the special 'Noble Rot' bacteria (called *Edelfaul* in German), acts upon these grapes by shrivelling the skins and concentrating the juice inside each berry. Such wines are intensely and lusciously perfumed, delicately fruity and usually surprisingly

GERMAN WINE LABELS: **1** *Qualitaetswein mit Pradikat* denotes the top category of German wine. Quality wines like this estate-bottled Rheinhessen wine state the parish or village name first, then the specific vineyard (*lage*) name, e.g. Niersteiner Paterberg (the suffix -er only appears when the village name is followed by the vineyard), as well as the grape variety and its manner of harvesting, e.g. Rülander Spaetlese. **2** An example of the second category of German wine, *Qualitaetswein* from defined regions: Piesport is one of the great Moselle wine villages and Goldtröpfchen an outstanding vineyard. **3** A different kind of *Qualitaetswein* from the Rheingau region; made from the noble Riesling grape, it comes from vineyards in the renowned district (*Bereich*) of Johannisberg. **4** Another district wine from Nierstein but only meriting the *Tafelwein* category, meaning German table wine without any particular specifications. **5** The popularity of Liebfraumilch (*see Glossary*), led to many hock-style wines appearing everywhere by this name. Under new wine laws, however, Liebfraumilch wines can now come only from vineyards in Rheinhessen, Nahe and the Palatinate, and many are sold under brand names. **6** Moselle wine from the village of Zeltingen sold under a proprietary name.

low in alcohol, although magnificent and large-scale in character and flavour. They are very expensive wines and should also be appraised at leisure, outside the context of a meal, on some very special occasion.

Eiswein (pronounce the first syllable to rhyme with 'ice'): In certain years, right at the end of the vintage, almost up to Christmas, frost will literally freeze the grapes on the vines overnight, and then they can be taken to be pressed while they are still actually coated with ice. The juice that flows from this pressing is concentrated and a curious, delicate and subtle wine results; it is very expensive and, as some growers never make an 'Icewine', they are rather rare.

Grape names Although formerly only a few varieties of grapes were used to make the great German wines, increasing use is being made of different varieties for various good reasons. Often the grape name is stated on labels, but sometimes, for the inexpensive wines, no grape names may be given. If the great Riesling grape is used for an inexpensive wine, this is usually proudly stated on the label, and it may also be assumed that for all the finest German wines the Riesling alone will be used.

Some very fine wines may also be made, however, from the acknowledged successful varieties, like Scheurebe, Silvaner, Traminer, and Mueller-Thurgau, even in the higher categories of quality, and these names will usually appear on a label as well.

Other information The only other bits of information on a German wine label may be that, with the finest wines, the number of the individual cask from which the wine was bottled is given, as the different casks are kept separate, unlike the overall vatting which is given to the finest French wines. The names of the vineyard and its owner should appear also; an owner may be an individual, or an establishment, such as the various *hospices* (charitable hospitals) endowed with vineyards, or the educational and religious bodies owning properties and the State Domain (the biggest grower of German wines); their names can be long and impressive, especially if the owner happens to have a title as well as a long name. But don't be put off by them as, once you begin to enjoy these fine wines, you'll find it becomes easier to remember the details of those that you have drunk.

Part Two

Wine and Food

Chapter 6 *Programming Wines*

The traditional order for serving wines, when more than one is involved, is: progress from dry to medium dry or sweet, serve young wines before old wines, and in general, serve white wines before red wines, and make the last wine served the outstanding one.

It is not difficult to see the logic of this progression. If you serve a sweet wine and then follow it with a dry one, the latter will taste acid and horrible. If you follow a red wine with a dryish white wine, then either the white wine will be dryer than the red and hence taste less good than it should, or else the white wine will be lighter in style than the red, making virtually no impression on the palate; usually, the red wine will be a fuller and more satisfying wine, so that the white wine that comes after it may seem thin and unattractive, whereas it would have appeared excellent, if served the other way round.

To serve an old wine before a young one is to risk the young wine seeming sharp and coarse, all the more so if the older wine is particularly fine. However, it is perfectly possible to serve a great sweet white wine after a red wine at the end of a meal, and also for this white wine to be a younger wine, for obviously you would not often serve this kind of wine with the meat course. Not that there is anything wrong in drinking a sweet or sweetish wine with the main course of a meal if you and your guests like to do this, but a sweet wine cuts the appetite more than a dry one.

Finally, the last impression made at even the humblest form of entertainment should always be the best, which is why it is wise to make the last wine served the most important, and this often means that it may be the most expensive. The great sweet wines are still bargains, because of the absurd fashion for dry wines, but, whether you are ending with a sweet white or a red wine, the last wine should give the impression of being the most expensive. Conversely, if you open a dinner with a magnificent wine, you may be hard put to it to serve anything better immediately afterwards – far better to work up to a climax. It is curious but true that if you are going to serve a good or great wine, it will always taste better if it is introduced by a more humble but good wine as this prepares the palate for the great one.

People with some experience of wine drinking often argue about these simple rules and sometimes experiment by breaking them. This is fine, providing you do not risk spoiling the enjoyment of your guests, and that you are not afraid to admit a mistake should your experiment go wrong. But, in general, the rules are founded on a pattern of wines which are generally most satisfactory and give the greatest pleasure to drinkers.

Consider the meal as a whole — It is no good getting several wines to accompany carefully-prepared dishes and then serving either apéritifs, which will ruin the impression that even the finest table wines can make, or (not quite so serious) an ill-chosen drink after the meal, which will spoil the overall impression of a perfectly-programmed dinner.

For example, if you drink an apéritif that is not bone-dry, then you will not enjoy a fine dry wine with the first course – better to serve no wine at all with this and go on to something with whatever you serve subsequent to the opening dish. One of the most flagrant errors constantly made in this way is to serve before a meal a medium sherry (remember, a lot of sherries are by no means bone-dry, even if they are listed as 'dry' on a wine list), white vermouth, or drink in which any sweet ingredient appears, and then follow them with a Chablis, young Moselle, or Muscadet; at best, none of these wines will taste particularly enjoyable, at worst they may simply seem acid to the drinker who does not realize why they do not please.

So plan your apéritifs as well as your wines – if you only serve one wine with a meal, then make sure this will follow on from whatever you were drinking beforehand.

How many wines to serve?

Many people become uneasy at the prospect of giving a dinner party, because of the number of wines they fear may be involved. In fact, this can be the least of the problems host or hostess has to solve – there need only be one! Of course, you can serve a range of varying wines (and spirits), but whether you do so or not is entirely up to you; it is as correct to serve a single drink as it is to serve half a dozen. Indeed, the discriminating guest will probably prefer one appropriate drink to several ill-assorted mixtures.

Making your decision — Decide, first of all, on your plan of action. Are you having the same wine all through, whatever kind of entertainment is planned, or are you going to serve a separate drink by way of apéritif, and then a wine with the meal (see Chapter 2 for the part apéritifs should play).

Your decision may be affected by the kind of meal you are proposing to offer: for example, at a buffet it is very much simpler to have one single drink for the whole party than several; in addition, at a meal where everyone sits down, you may be entertaining a number of people and serving several kinds of drink, which may involve your washing up glasses half way through the meal. Expense, too, has to be considered; it is always better to have enough bottles of one well-chosen, albeit modest, wine than a rationed portion of several expensive ones.

Serving one wine The points above show how, if you wish, you can serve the same kind of drink before a meal and also with most food: this is a dry or medium dry wine, which, in the circumstances, will probably be white. It can be still or sparkling, which, in the case of the latter, is likely to be the more expensive of the two, but you can, nevertheless, choose wines in the inexpensive, medium and top price ranges which will suit this kind of occasion.

Serving two wines The most usual number of wines or drinks served when one is being hospitable is two: an apéritif and a wine with the food. The apéritif can also accompany the first course of the meal, if there are going to be three or more courses.

If you plan to offer apéritifs which are quite different from the drinks with which you accompany the meal, then you must make up your mind whether you are going to offer guests a selection of these – such as different spirit-based drinks or cocktails – or whether you are simply going to offer them a different type of wine, whether still, sparkling or fortified. Again, the choice is up to you. It is always easier, however, simply to give people the choice of one drink and a non-alcoholic alternative, rather than to try and show off by offering several different sorts of mixtures, unless these are very simple, like gin and French (dry vermouth), vermouth with soda, gin and tonic, pink gin (with Angostura Aromatic Bitters), or sherry, white port, or dry Madeira. For special occasions, a glass of a dry or dryish sparkling wine is ideal.

Unless people are going to spend a long time drinking before the meal, then, if they really do not like the drink you offer, they can toy with it for half an hour and need not have more, whereas if you offer them a selection of spirit-based drinks, wine and wine-based apéritifs, you will find that, at the end of the evening, you have spent a lot of money and your guests may well have consumed more than they really need. It is a debatable point as to whether too much to drink is worse than too little but neither is good.

Serving three wines This is becoming quite a convention with what one might describe as 'company fare' – meals to which one devotes a little extra attention in order to do your guests proud. There will be an apéritif, a wine to accompany the first course and then another one to drink for the rest of the meal.

In many ways this is admirable, but there are some circumstances in which the balance of the wines seems quite wrong: if the first course is food unsuited to wine (see page 126), then it is obviously mere ostentation to serve a wine just for the sake of serving a different drink at this stage in the meal; also, should the first course be a comparatively light one, such as cold consommé or a cream soup, which don't call for wine, then it is really not necessary to have any specific drink with this course at all. In such instances it is often both easier and more acceptable to carry the apéritif over to the first course (should people wish to go on drinking), providing it is a table wine or something that can acceptably be drunk with food, such as certain types of sherry, vermouth, or virtually anything except a spirit-based mixed drink.

You can then have your second wine at the end of the meal – either with fruit or a fruity pudding, or afterwards, quite by itself before the coffee is served. This has the advantage of doing away with the necessity for serving liqueurs (which can also be expensive) after the meal, and can prolong the hospitality pleasantly but not extravagantly. If you concentrate on the drinks at the beginning of the meal and do not serve anything later on, then there is often a feeling of anticlimax. Of course, if you have a range of liqueurs and some brandy anyway, then the problem does not exist.

Serving four wines This may sound a lot, but if you count the apéritif as one, and plan to serve a dessert wine or perhaps a wine after the meal, then it is not markedly lavish to serve two wines to accompany a fairly formal luncheon or dinner. The most usual arrangement is to have a white wine and a red one. In fact two table wines are part of the catering for many family meals, such as the traditional Christmas one, which is usually based on some kind of roast poultry, when some of the company may prefer to drink a white wine throughout, although others will prefer red, as is reasonable enough with anything roast.

But you don't have to serve one white and one red wine unless you want to. Instead, you may prefer to serve two red wines, whose comparison can be extremely interesting, and especially if the first course doesn't call for wine (such as a cream soup or something with eggs), then it is often both interesting and convenient as regards calculating quantities to have a pair of wines served simultaneously with what may be described as the main course of the meal.

If you do this pairing, then choose wines from the same region – it somehow jolts the palate to have to make the transition between, say, claret and Burgundy in this way, and, if you wish to study the two wines, then you will be able to make a far more reasonable appraisal of them if they are similar in style. Of course, it is perfectly possible to serve a pair of white wines in this way as well, although if there is any doubt, probably all but the most fanatical white wine enthusiasts would agree on choosing red.

More than four wines By now you can appreciate that it is possible to serve the most important kind of guests with a single wine and, without showing off, to pamper the family and close friends at an informal meal with as many as four. The choice is entirely up to you. But if you serve more than four wines, including whatever you serve as an apéritif and at the end of or after the meal, then the decision to do this presupposes that the meal is going to be quite lengthy, and that the guests will probably want to discuss the wines with some seriousness; this need not mean that the conversation is dull, for the only kind of wine talk that is really dull is that emanating from those who are both pompous and ignorant! The enthusiasts will make the subject entertaining. Nor do you need a very long and complicated sort of meal: some of the most enjoyable 'wine' dinners can consist of a very simple first course, with some form of roast meat to follow, and cheese and fruit afterwards, but there may well be four or even five different clarets served during the course of such a meal!

However, by the time you want to serve as many wines as this, you will probably be fairly knowledgeable about wine or have made friends with several wine merchants, so that their detailed advice and your experience will guide you. Simply to serve a lot of different wines does not necessarily mean a memorable experience for the wine drinker and, as with cooking, it is always best to offer something about which you are sure rather than to risk a failure (unless you are entertaining friends who can be relied on to be understanding and indulgent).

Incidentally, if you are serving two or more wines for direct comparison and appraisal, remember to make it easy for your guests not to confuse the glasses. You will, of course, serve fine wines in glasses appropriate to them as regards shape and size (see Chapter 7) but, should the glasses be identical, then differentiate them, either by making a mark on the foot of the glass or attaching a small identifying tag to the stem. People can exercise their own judgment as to whether they prefer to drink 'from right to left' or 'from left to right' in relation to the table positioning of the glasses, and whether they help themselves or whether the wine is poured for them, it should be made perfectly clear as to which bottle or decanter is directed into which glass. At a meal of this kind, you don't want to have suddenly to produce a cup!

Choosing table wines

Many people try to be very particular in choosing wines with foods, refusing to realize that, as wines themselves vary so much, it is risky to lay down hard and fast rules as to what goes with what. Also, vintage wines can vary greatly so that a wine perfectly suited to accompany a specific dish from one vintage may really be inappropriate from another. Then there is the problem of shopping; no one single shop can, at all times, have a complete range of the wines of the world, and the customer who has to make the best of the available resources can be discouraged if told that only a particular type of wine is the appropriate choice with a certain sort of food. So, be reassured: if you follow certain basic, sensible rules, you can then choose appropriate wines from virtually any source of supply. As your experience grows, you should start to experiment a little, and eventually you will choose wine with complete assurance. Remember that wine is a food as well, and try always to look on the choice of wine with food as something fascinating and enjoyable rather than a difficult problem.

Wine's role with food

The overall piece of advice which is likely to be of most use is that **wine should either complement or contrast with the dish**. This means that if you have a very rich fish dish, such as turbot, halibut or salmon with a creamy sauce, then the wine that will be most enjoyable with this will either be a very crisp dry one, or something with a certain amount of fatness to it as well. The same goes for meat, poultry and game: for example, in Alsace, where goose is often eaten, a crisp, fruity Alsatian white wine might be served, but in other wine regions where geese abound a very full-bodied red wine might be preferred. Although dishes which have regional origins tend to be associated with the local wines, this does not mean, however, that you must have, say, a wine from the south of France simply because you are going to serve ratatouille, or an Italian wine with a pasta dish. Certainly it makes the choice easier if you *can* partner regional foods and wines but, if this is difficult, then try and find out what the appropriate regional wine is like and match this up with a similar style of wine from some other wine region.

So you see that, according to what you yourself prefer, it is not only possible to choose rather full-bodied, assertive wines with some foods, but also those wines which are virtually the opposite in style; either way you can be equally satisfied. The one thing to avoid, however, is to pick a wine that is very light in character when you are serving something rich or assertive in flavour, because this will, obviously, be overwhelmed by the food; for example, if you are having steak and kidney pudding or a rich stew, it would be absurd to choose a rosé wine, as most of these are far too light in character to give the impression of drinking anything except a vaguely alcoholic beverage. The wine has its part to play as well as the food. Some of the more delicate wines, like the finest German white wines, tend to be overwhelmed in this way and, similarly, certain great clarets can hardly be appraised and tasted to advantage if they are served at the same time with a very spicy dish, or something like pizza.

Try to keep the wines generally consistent with the food, choosing good but fairly simple dishes with the finer wines, and more everyday wines with everyday recipes. If you have spent a lot of money on your food, then it is unfair to expect a very cheap bottle of wine to make any kind of impression, but a good bottle, of modest or high price, can make bread and cheese into a meal fit for any company.

Recommendations as to wine and food partnerships often include the advice 'white wines with fish and white meat, red wines with red'. It is perfectly true that many people do not like red wine with fish, although most would enjoy a dry rosé with simple fish dishes. However, do not think that it is impossible to enjoy red wine with fish – although you should avoid making the experiment unless you can do it in your family circle or with friends who will not be offended if the combination of flavours is not really liked. So, in general, the choice for fish dishes is a white wine, not too sweet, but varying in style, of course, according to the fish and the way it is cooked.

As for white meat, just how 'white' do people assume a turkey, with all the trimmings, to be! The strong flavourings of stuffing, rich gravy, bacon rolls, and any additional sauces make this a rich dish, and if you want to accompany it with a white wine, then it must be a full-bodied one, such as a fairly fine white Burgundy, or something like a Spanish-bottled white Rioja, which is able to withstand the strong and varied flavours of the food.

Many people serve a red wine with any type of roast or grilled meat, poultry and, of course, game, but this is a personal preference. If you want to drink white wines with red meat, then do so, but make sure they are large-scale white wines, which won't be swamped by the food. In Germany quite often the great hocks are drunk in this way, for, of course if you live in a region that produces only white wine, then it is natural to drink this with virtually everything; the reverse is true as regards red wine. You have only to think of the way in which people in wine-producing regions, where red, white and rosé are freely available, choose their wines entirely according to what they feel like drinking, to realize that much of our particularization about what should go with what is rather unnecessary.

Another point to bear in mind is that in every category of the major wines of the world, both red and white, there is usually a choice from dry to medium sweet or even very sweet, from very light and delicate to full-bodied and, indeed, definitely assertive, from crisp and refreshing to rich, well-flavoured, and almost meatily satisfying. Only experience can give you the know-how to choose the kind of wine you want, but there really is a wine for every dish.

Sparkling wines can, of course, be served with food as well (see Chapter 2). But it is just worth bearing in mind that, as the charm of most of these wines is their freshness and, with the finest wines, delicacy, they can sometimes be a little overwhelmed by some foods. Also, they can be a little too lively for some people to drink throughout a meal; even in the Champagne region itself, it is quite usual for a hostess to serve Champagne throughout the meal up to the cheese course, when she may then very well offer a red wine. It is a matter dictated by the preferences and digestions of those who are going to eat and drink.

Enemies of wine

There are some foods that do not partner any wine particularly well. This may either be because they are of a very strong flavour, or because they completely alter the sense of taste, so that, although wine may be drunk with such foods, it is rather a waste to serve anything but an ordinary, everyday wine.

Curry, or any spiced foods, or those accompanied by a strongly-flavoured curry sauce, virtually kill the taste of wine. If you must drink a wine, then choose something ordinary and fairly robust, either red or white, but it is probably better to serve beer or cider.

Chinese or Japanese food: The delicate flavours and complex sauces are usually quite sufficiently interesting to the Occidental palate to make any accompanying wine superfluous. Again, either a not too-assertive or delicate red or white wine (the latter is likely to be the most suitable) may be served, if you are not going to drink the wines of the respective countries which are themselves strange to many westerners.

Salads: Vinegar is an enemy of wine, so serving wine with salads is often condemned because the vinegar in the dressing will affect its taste. But this can rather depend on the amount of vinegar used: if you make a French dressing using only two or three parts of oil to one of vinegar, then, of course, the vinegar will predominate and tend to make any wine taste sour and, indeed, seem to turn it to vinegar in your mouth. A French dressing of, say, not less than five parts of oil to one of vinegar may not seriously affect an ordinary table wine in this context.

It is also worth remembering that, in countries such as France, the salad is served at the end of the principal fish or meat course, instead of with it, and the wine will either have been finished by this stage of the meal, or there will be a pause before people go on to the cheese with which they will finish the contents of their wine glasses.

Salady dishes at the very beginning of a meal need not be accompanied by a wine at all, or, if you want to start with something piquant of this nature, then try to provide a 'blotting paper' course, such as clear or cream soup, to come after it and before a dish with which a good wine is to be served. Pickles, chutney, anything with a lot of pepper or spice, sweet-sour dishes, all make it extremely difficult to taste anything else and, therefore, no delicate wine should be served with them.

Egg dishes: Anything in which there is a preponderance of eggs, especially egg yolk, makes it difficult to appreciate any wine properly, unless it is a robust one. You know how egg yolk coats and sticks to a spoon – it does exactly the same to the palate, and many wines can taste curiously metallic after eating egg. This is why a fairly assertive type of wine, nothing too delicate and nothing too fine, should be chosen to accompany an egg dish, if you want to drink wine, and, if an egg-based sauce is to be served, the same caution should be observed with regard to choosing the wine.

Chocolate, however, is the real palate-stunner. It coats the palate and seems to remain on it for literally hours afterwards. This is why it is virtually a waste to serve any wine with a dish containing chocolate, although a chocolate-based liqueur can be very enjoyable.

Citrus fruits, and in particular oranges, because of their acidity, and certain other fruits, such as bananas, can make it difficult to enjoy any wine at the same time.

Although the chart (*pages 128–129*) will enable you to pick out what food goes with what wine, there are several general points to bear in mind when making your choice.

Some first courses have a traditional accompaniment – with caviare, for example, it is vodka – but Champagne or other quality dry sparkling wine, or a very dry white wine are also acceptable. The same applies to fish pâtés and mousses, and if any spirit is included in a recipe such as malt whisky in a kipper pâté, then it is probably best to serve this with the food in preference to wine.

With melon or other fruity first courses, there is no need to serve wine at all, although some people like a dry white wine, or a little white or tawny port with melon, often putting it in the fruit (there is nothing against this – but many people might prefer the wine in a glass, to drink).

With foie gras and rich meat pâtés the choice is very wide. Some people even recommend a luscious sweet white wine, but this depends greatly on the other drinks to be served. Most people would probably find a medium dry or very dry white wine, still or sparkling, the acceptable partner, but take care to match the quality of the wine to the food – do not partner fine foie gras, for example, with an everyday dry wine.

With shellfish and crustaceans, traditionally very dry white wines, such as Muscadet or Chablis, are served, but there is no need to stick rigidly to these; if you are eating dressed crab or if mayonnaise is served with the shellfish, then a dryish wine of medium quality is probably best, as the dressing will otherwise swamp a delicate wine. Choose a fresh, crisp wine, whether very dry or medium dry, that you know and that is in keeping with the quality of the food; in other words, with oysters, lobster, scampi or langouste, serve a fullish-flavoured, fine white wine, and with clams, prawns, shrimps, whelks, winkles and cockles a good medium quality wine.

Simple Conventional Partnerships of Wine and Food

Type of Course or Food	No wine at all	Dry Vermouth	Champagne/Sparkling Dry	Champagne/Sparkling Medium	Champagne/Sparkling Sweet	White Dry Full-bodied	White Dry Light-bodied	White Medium	Red Sweet	Red Full-bodied	Red Light-bodied	Rosé Dry–Medium	Sherry Dry/Fino	Sherry Medium/Amontillado	Sherry Sweet	Port Dry	Port White	Port Sweet	Madeira Dry–Medium	Madeira Sweet	Marsala Dry	Marsala Sweet	Brandy	Liqueurs	Vodka	Others
Apéritif		§§	§§	§§			§§	§§					§§	§§		§§	§§		§§		§§		§§			
Egg dishes	+							++				++														
Salads and Piquant dishes	+							++				++														
Avocado pears							+	+				‡‡														
Melon and Fruit first courses	+						++																			
Soup – clear/consommé	+												§§	§§					§§		§§					
Soup – thick/cream	+													§§					§§							
Soup – bisque/enriched with brandy	+																									
Caviare			†*			†*																			§§	
Fish – pâté/mousse			†*			†*																				
Fish – with spirit included in it	+																									
Foie gras and Meat pâté (match quality with wine)			§§	§§		§§	§§																§§			
Shellfish and Crustacea (match quality with wine)			+			*†	*†	§§																		§§
Fish – smoked			+			†	+	*†																		
Fish – fried						‡	‡‡	‡																		
Fish – delicate, plainly served						*†	*†	*†				++														

Food		
– delicate, with sauce	*†	
– fat rich	*†	*†	*†
Meat – roasts, plain	*†	*†	*†
– roasts, with sauce	†	†	
– grills, plain	*†	†*	*
– grills, with piquant foods, egg and bacon included		†	
– casseroles and stews (including pies, suet puddings, hot pot)	‡‡	‡‡	
– cold cooked (match quality with wine)	§§	§§	§§
– boiled	*†	*†	*†
– made-up (including rissoles, croquettes, mince etc.)		†	†
Game – casseroles and stews		‡‡	‡‡
– fine game and roasts	*	*†	*†
– cold cooked (match quality with wine)	§§	§§	§§
Poultry – roast	*†	*†	*
– poached and boiled	†	†	†
– grilled	‡‡	‡‡	†
– casseroles	‡‡	‡‡	†
Cheese – mild/soft and creamy	*	*†	*†
– strong/hard and matured/blue		*†	*†
Sweet course and Puddings		‡‡	‡‡
Dessert fruit/nuts and After meal drinks			*†
Chinese food	‡‡	‡‡	‡‡
Curry/Spiced or Strongly-flavoured dishes or Devilled foods	‡‡	‡‡	‡‡

KEY TO SYMBOLS
*= Fine wine   †= Medium quality   ‡= Everyday, inexpensive wine   §= Any kind

To accompany delicate fish, such as sole, plaice, scallops, or any flat fish plainly served, the classic white wines of medium to fine quality, but not too sweet, are ideal. If the sauces with the fish are of an assertive flavour, then a more robust white wine is probably better, or something very fruity, with a little more sweetness to it.

With any fat, full-flavoured fish, such as turbot, halibut, salmon, or salmon-trout, a white wine of dry or medium dry style and full-bodied character is ideal. Choose from one of the classic wines, or, with a regional recipe, a regional wine of the same style, if possible.

If there is to be wine included in the dish, whether it be poached or boiled poultry or a casserole or stew of meat or the humbler forms of game, such as rabbit, hare, pigeon, or grouse and similar birds, then the same wine is usually the best one to drink with it.

With cold cooked meats, your choice of wine will be dictated by the type of meal you are giving, whether this is to be a buffet, a picnic, or a luncheon, or a supper. If you are serving salad, then the wine should not be too fine or delicate; if the meat is of prime quality, and the accompanying vegetables simple, then a fine wine is advisable – and this applies also to cold cooked game.

It is generally agreed that roast meat and game taste at their best when partnered by red wine, and the finer the dish, the finer the wine. However, always take into consideration any additional sauces or stuffings because their strong flavours may mean that you should choose a more robust wine. With the finer types of game, the finest red wines are always appropriate – claret, red Burgundy, or red Rhône. True, in many regions in Germany a great white wine will be served, but, for drinkers outside specific wine regions, a red wine is usually liked best. Red Burgundy is rather traditional with venison, although there are certainly plenty of large-scale, great clarets which are equally good partners.

With roast poultry, a red wine is usually most acceptable to the majority, unless a white is preferred on all occasions. If so, then the white wine must be fairly robust. The red wine can be of any quality, but, if the bird is one that makes a lot of fat, such as a goose or duckling, then a certain crispness and freshness in the wine is desirable, so as to set this off.

All wine goes well with cheese, but especially red wine. This is why in many European countries, the cheese is served before the sweet course, so that any red wine accompanying the main course can be finished – after the sweet it is impossible to return and appreciate the contents of one's wine glass. If the wines with the meal you have selected tend to be delicate, then avoid serving very strong cheeses, such as some of the blue cheeses and the hard matured British cheeses. With the finer and more delicate red wines, opt for creamy cheeses or the mild hard or semi-matured cheeses.

Very few people want to drink a wine with any type of pudding today, and if the pudding, such as a trifle, is enriched with liqueur, or has a lot of eggs and cream in it, or contains a large quantity of chocolate, then it really is a waste to serve any wine by way of an accompaniment. If, on a special occasion, such as a birthday, you want to serve something to drink, perhaps at the proposing of a toast, then a medium to sweet wine, and preferably a sparkling wine for a celebration, is ideal.

You can serve Champagne, or a good quality sparkling wine, all through a meal. This can be very agreeable at a buffet meal, a light meal, such as an after-theatre supper, or a luxurious type of picnic. But sparkling wines served through a fairly formal meal including rich dishes, can be taxing for the digestion of some people, so that it is advisable to offer another wine, perhaps a red wine with the cheese, if you are going to have a number of courses.

When in doubt Stick to a conventional arrangement of wines with food, especially when you are entertaining guests whose tastes may not be as adventurous as your own, or when you are yourself nervous as to whether all will go well. Keep your experimental sessions for close friends, who won't mind if something goes wrong and who will tell you frankly if they do not like the combinations of wines and foods that you have selected.

Don't, when you are entertaining your in-laws to be, your husband's boss and his wife, or your rich relations, try to be clever with an obscure little wine, just because it is unknown and cheap – it may be dreary and nasty, and one of your guests may know enough about wine and your particular choice to be able to tell you exactly why you shouldn't have chosen it! But don't play perennially safe, by only choosing the well-known advertised branded wines, which everybody will know. However good these are, it makes an occasion more interesting if you can discuss the contents of the bottle – remember always that it is never rude to criticize a wine. And, as long as people linger over the contents of their glasses with appreciation and interest, so long will there be unending discussions as to what is exactly the perfect solution to the insoluble problem of what goes with what.

Chapter 7 *The Practicalities of Wine Drinking*

Many people are under the impression that to enjoy a wide range of wine, they should also possess a wide range of glasses of different shapes and sizes. This is not necessary at all; the ideal wine glass is also the all-purpose wine glass and can be bought quite easily, at prices ranging from pence to pounds for each one. But it is worth while having the correct shape and size – there are possible variations on these – simply because the right shape will make the wine taste, smell and look better. Selection of the right size also means that, not only can you serve virtually any wine, sparkling or still, in this glass, but also, if you are having a party, you will find that people who have their drinks poured into fairly generously-sized glasses will usually not drink as much as if the unsatisfactory small ones are used; small glasses tend to be emptied rapidly and therefore have to be topped up more often. It is, therefore, both 'right' and an economy to choose the ideal glass.

The ideal wine glass — Wine gives pleasure by its colour, its smell and its taste, therefore any glass from which it is drunk should display all these assets to the best advantage.

The glass should be plain so that the colour of the wine, whether red or white, can be enjoyed by the eye. Tinted glasses are a relic of the days when the production of wine was somewhat haphazard and bits might be found floating in the wine; these would not necessarily affect the flavour, but our squeamish ancestors did not like to see them, hence the use of tinted glasses. Nowadays, the beautiful colour of a limpid wine should be enjoyed without any colour screen getting in the way, and tinted glasses are really only suitable for water and soft drinks.

Cut glass is a beautiful thing to have on the table and cut crystal or engraved crystal is an illumination to any place setting, but the lover of good wine usually prefers a perfectly plain glass, at least as far as the bowl of the glass is concerned; cutting necessarily involves a fairly thick glass and the thinner the glass or crystal, the greater the pleasure of drinking fine wine from it.

The wine glasses (as opposed to water goblets, carafes and decanters) used on the tables of members of the wine trade tend to be perfectly plain and of thin glass, or, in the luxurious category, crystal so thin that a slight pressure of the hand will make the glass give perceptibly.

The stem: The ideal wine glass is on a stem, whether it is tall or short. This is so that the refreshing coolness of a white or rosé wine will not be affected by the heat of the drinker's hand. If you have the opportunity to watch members of the wine trade drinking wine or people whose experience of wine is considerable, you will see how they very seldom hold a glass by the bowl, but pick it up by the stem or even hold it by the foot. This makes it easier to swing the wine around in the glass and thereby release the beautiful fragrance, which is one of the charms of wine drinking.

The shape of the ideal wine glass enables the drinker to smell the wine. It is astonishing how many elegant glasses are designed so that any smell the drink may have is, almost deliberately, directed away from the nose! It should be retained in the bowl of the glass, allowed to develop and then, as it were, 'introduced' to the drinker's nose. This means that the bowl of the glass will be shaped either like an elongated tulip, or like an onion with the top chopped off, or possibly what may be described as an elongated rectangle with slightly curved corners.

Ideally, the rim of the glass should be slightly narrower than the widest point of the bowl, but if the sides go straight up, this does not greatly matter. What is unfortunate is when the sides of any wine glass spread outwards to a pronounced extent – a slight outward angle does not matter too much, but a sharp one merely means that it is impossible to swirl the wine around without risking a spill and the smell (for which one has paid after all) escapes without getting to the nose.

The size of the ideal wine glass should be reasonable, because, in order to swirl the wine around to release the fragrance for appreciation, it is definitely incorrect to fill any glass to the brim with wine. Half-way up or, at most two-thirds, is the maximum level to which the wine should be poured. Some people have been cheated all their drinking lives of the wonderful bouquet of sherry, simply because they have always been obliged to drink it in a tiny little glass, filled up to the top!

In terms of capacity, a $5\frac{1}{2}$ – 6 fl. oz glass is about right for everything, but glasses for the great red wines may well be between 8–10 fl. oz. It is not, however, necessary to have giant glasses, even for Burgundy or brandy, as not only are these out of proportion and aesthetically unsightly, but they can

Glasses for sparkling wines: **1** Traditional Champagne flute; **2** Elongated tulip; and **3** Saucer – a poor shape as it lets the bubbles and bouquet escape too quickly.

4 Copita or traditional sherry glass; **5** All-purpose fortified wine glass (about 3 fl. oz); **6, 7** and **8** Popular sherry glasses but unsuitably shaped as they let the bouquet escape.

9 All-purpose tulip shape; 10 All-purpose goblet; 11 Traditional shape for Alsatian and German wines; 12 Traditional Rhine wine glass with chunky stem.

13 Balloon glass for fine red Burgundy and brandy; 14 A variation on the tulip shape ideal for table wines and brandy; 15 Traditional claret glass.

aerate the wine or the brandy too much, resulting in the bouquet or fragrance being thrown off too sharply and dissipated in the goldfish bowl-like glass before it can even get to the drinker. Moderation in all things is a good precept with regard to wine as in other aspects of gastronomy.

You can buy the ideal wine glass at almost any chain store or shop that sells the cheapest type of glass. It is also possible to buy crystal glasses of the ideal shape which will cost several pounds apiece. But, given the right type of glass as regards shape and capacity, absence of colour and general proportions, the same glass can be used for every single type of table wine, red, white and pink, for all sparkling wines, for port, sherry, Madeira and any other fortified wine, for brandy, including Cognac and Armagnac, for most liqueurs (of course the helping will be small, but this does not matter), and for mixed drinks.

If you want to vary the glasses you set for wines, which indeed is a pleasant thing to do, then there are certain types of glass, traditional in various wine regions, which are quite easy to get: tall bulbous glasses on brown or green stems are associated with Rhine wines and Moselle, and Alsatian wines respectively; the short-stemmed elongated tulip, sometimes known as a *copita* (the Spanish word means 'little mouthful'), is used in the sherry region; in the Champagne district and other areas where sparkling wine is made, very tall glasses, rather like elongated trumpets are sometimes used. There are many other examples of attractive glasses which, those who make the wines believe, show off their products particularly well.

But the basic wine glass, as described above, is always correct and if you want to vary it, should you serve more than one wine at a time, then it is perhaps a good idea to have one set of glasses in the goblet shape and another tulip-shaped, so as to mark a difference. Unfortunately, people shopping for glasses are frequently told that small ones, of really the wrong shape for showing off the wine, heavily cut, and possibly even coloured are right for certain different types of wines. If you have been given a 'suite' of expensive glasses of this sort, and the donor visits you frequently, it is obviously difficult to avoid using them – but perhaps you can keep them for occasions when the finest wines are not going to be served. Otherwise, glasses of this sort are really only suitable for cocktails or the sort of spirits – such as neat vodka, schnapps, ouzo, or pick-me-ups such as Fernet Branca – which do not really need to be tasted. Use such glasses for little flower posies or, if they are big enough, for water goblets.

Care of glasses It is surprising how many people who prize and respect the beautiful things that they set on their table are nevertheless careless about caring for glasses. It is important to take some trouble about this, because it is a frequent happening that wine is rejected as 'bad' when, in fact, it is the fault of either the glass or the cloth with which it has been dried. If you do not rinse your glasses after washing them, and if any detergent remains in the glass, it can make the wine poured into the glass on any subsequent occasion taste horrible and may make even the finest Champagne turn a revolting orange-pink colour!

The same applies to a drying cloth – because of course fine glass does need to be polished, even if it does not require drying, once you have rinsed it in very hot water, when it can be simply left to drain. If the cloth used for polishing glasses is also used for drying dishes and any grease or food is clinging to it, then this can also make the glass smell, and if the glass cloth itself has been washed in detergent and insufficiently rinsed, then it will also effect the glass. Does all this sound a lot of trouble about something trivial? But wine is a beautiful thing and to reject a bottle that tastes less good than it should, simply because you haven't rinsed the glass cloth sufficiently, can lead to great disappointment – or even ruin a dinner party. Our grandmothers, who had special glass cloths, not used for anything else, were wise about this.

Another small precaution in caring for glasses is how they are put away: if you turn them upside down, certainly dust will be kept out of them, but at the same time they tend to take on the smell of either the lining of the shelf on which they rest or any wood or paint on this, and when they are used this smell will also affect the wine. It is astonishing how nasty a fine wine can taste when it has to compete with the smell of even the best plastic shelf covering, which has been captured in the bowl of the glass! Unless you can wash your glasses every time before you use them, it is better to store them the right side up, so that the air can circulate freely; if you must turn them upside down in a cupboard or on a shelf, then do try to check that the surface with which they are in contact has no odour about it of any kind.

Decanters and carafes A beautiful decanter or elegant carafe, or even a fine jug, can set off a fine wine and its use on the table can make even an ordinary wine look better and, interestingly, taste really good. There are no rules about the choice of these, and the art of the glass cutter and engraver has been employed in past centuries so as to make antique decanters beautiful examples of glass and crystal at its finest. Decanters that are to be used for wine usually have a neck, so that it is easy to pour the wine and sometimes there are 'claret jugs' which, of course, can be used for other wine than the red wines of Bordeaux. The chunkier type of decanter is more usually associated with spirits. Decanters of a vaguely triangular shape are known as 'ship' decanters, because they were more stable than the other types, and therefore were practical for use aboard ship in former times.

Cleaning Ideally, decanters should always be cleaned immediately after they have
decanters been used. This does away with any likelihood of red wine in them staining
the bottom of the decanter. It is not difficult to remove this stain but it is a
nuisance to have to do this immediately before the decanter is required for
use again. If you should have forgotten a little wine in the bottom of a
decanter and it has stained the glass, then this can be easily lifted by the use
of a solution of Milton, or diluted bleach in water, which should be allowed
to stand in the decanter and then thoroughly rinsed out; the importance
of this rinsing is great and it is advisable to run the clean decanter under the
tap for several minutes at least so that all trace of the cleaning agent is completely removed.

The decanter should, after use or after cleaning, be allowed to drain so
that the inside is completely dry. If you are in a hurry, then dry it by either
standing it over a gentle source of heat, so that any moisture will drain away
and the interior be completely dried out, or else wrap a glass cloth around
the stick of a mop or a skewer, and use this to blot up any liquid inside. This
is important, because even a very small amount of stale water in a decanter
can make the whole thing smell stagnant when you come to use it again, and
it is obviously difficult to get rid of this immediately before you want to pour
wine into it, when you are probably in a hurry anyway.

Put the decanter away both clean and dry, with any stopper only lightly
inserted. If the stopper of an antique decanter does get stuck, and you cannot
remove this by gently turning this yourself, trickle a little oil around it and
see if this will shift it. Should this not work, then try running the neck of the
decanter – not the stopper – under the hot tap, so that the glass may expand
very slightly and release it. If all else fails, then get a chemist friend or someone in a laboratory to use one of the special holders they have for extracting
the stoppers of glass containers.

Storing wine and the mini-cellar

However cheap a bottle of wine may be, it will nevertheless have cost
you money and it is therefore silly to give it less than reasonable care once
you have got it home. But 'reasonable care' does not necessarily involve a
large amount of space and special conditions, such as a large cellar – although
how lucky you are if you have one. As nearly all wine, from the very cheapest
to the very finest, will provide more enjoyment if it is properly kept and,
ideally not drunk the same day that you have brought it home from the shop
(unless you have chosen a really inexpensive branded wine), it is worth
planning for a small amount of space to be always available in your home,
even if this is a bed-sitting room or tiny flat.

Glass decanters show off all good red wines; the wine funnel (rarely seen today) allows the wine to strike the side of the decanter instead of dropping to the bottom.

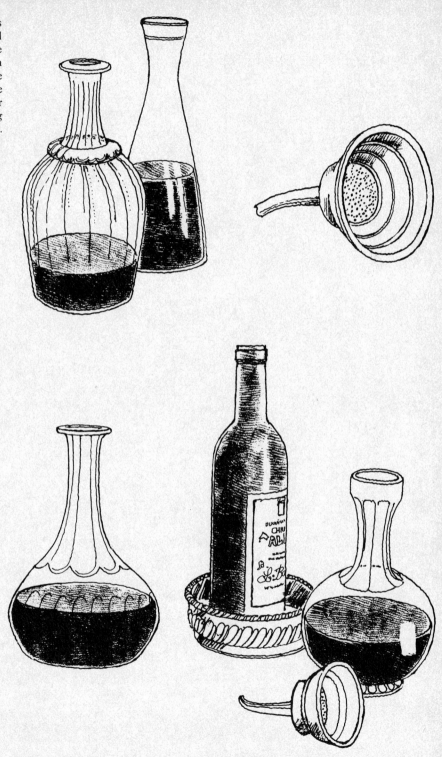

How to store wine All bottles of wine should be stored lying down on their sides, so that the cork in the bottle is kept moist and swollen and therefore cannot become dry and possibly let air in and, even, wine out. (Spirits, on the other hand, should always be kept upright, because the spirit can cause the cork or any stopper to deteriorate in time). If, wherever you put your bottles, you also take care to make a habit of keeping them with the labels uppermost, you can then easily see what you are pulling out of your mini-cellar.

Wine bins of many kinds are widely available, in metal or wood, to hold as few as half a dozen or a dozen bottles, or several dozen. Probably the most satisfactory and the cheapest are those which can be tailored to fit any place where you are going to have your wine in the home, taking the minimum of space. These bins can be made to your particular order by Farrow & Jackson Ltd., 41 Prescot Street, London E.1., and W. R. Loftus, 1 Charlotte Street, London W.1. The bins are not particularly handsome, but neither are they obtrusive and they will fit into many awkward corners if you are really short of space.

Where to store your wine Wines like dark, quiet, and a fairly constant temperature. Ideally, they prefer to rest in a coolish place, and the perfect cellar is probably one which is kept at about 10°C (50°F), or 13°C (55°F), and is not too dry. But, in fact, it will not matter very much if the temperature is a little higher than this providing – and this is really important – it does not vary greatly. If there is a rise in temperature in the summer of 10°C or more and a drop in the winter, the wine will not like or benefit from these ups and downs. This is why you should not store your wine in any place that gets a lot of direct sunlight, or where electric light shines constantly on the bottles, or in close proximity to any central heating, hot water pipes (such as a cupboard), or under a roof which is not insulated against the outside temperatures. Also, to be on the safe side, you should not keep bottles in close proximity to anything which has a strong smell, such as disinfectant, strings of onions hanging up, household cleaning material, or containers for oil or paraffin.

But it is not difficult to find a place for the bottles, even if your 'bin' is merely the cardboard carton in which they come, which, stood on one side, makes a perfect small-scale storage unit, if you have no permanent rack. Cupboards under stairs, the bottom of a larder, or perhaps underneath some cabinet or in the corner of a hall or passage are other possibilities. If you really are doubtful about finding a satisfactory place, then a wine merchant can probably arrange to store the wine for you, but this means that you will have to advise him when you want to take any away from your reserve; it is probably better, therefore, to keep only your special bottles in this way and have a permanent small stock of wines for everyday use in your home, which will only be kept there for a few months at a time at most.

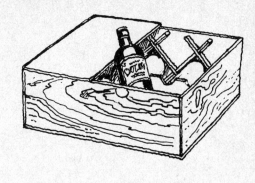

Different kinds of
racks for storing
wine

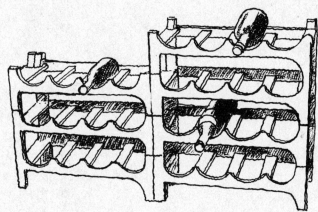

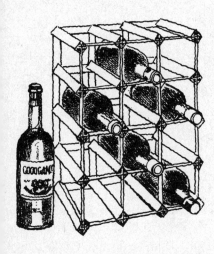

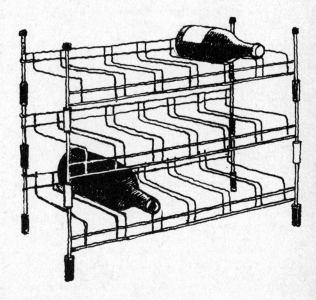

Bin order   If possible, always keep your wines with the white wines at the bottom of the bin, below the red wines, because the bottom, whether this is floor level or hip height, will be slightly cooler. Don't store wine high up at the top of a kitchen cupboard, simply because this does tend to get warm and, if you do have bottles sticking out of a bin at floor level, be sure that the necks do not protrude in the path of anyone mopping a floor or where children or animals can knock against them – if a neck of a bottle comes off, there can be a terrible mess and someone can cut themselves badly.

Keeping wine   A wine merchant will store wine for you by arrangement, but usually a small
at a wine   charge is made for doing this. As some merchants' cellars for customers'
merchant   reserves are not 'under the shop' at their premises, it is often necessary to advise when you want to take out bottles for drinking. The advantage of keeping wine in a merchant's cellars is that the conditions are ideal and, if you have bought young wines which you will be leaving to mature for some time, the fact that these are perfectly kept is a great advantage, both to you when you come to drink them and if by chance you wish to sell them later on. But usually you will have to store a dozen bottles at a time, although sometimes this can be a mixed case lot. In any event it is always worth while enquiring from the merchant when you are buying more wine than you can store in your own home.

Cellar   However you keep your stock of wine, there are several pieces of basic equip-
equipment   ment which it is always worth while having either in a box or drawer near to the 'cellar' or somewhere apart, so that you can always be sure of finding them even if you are in a hurry. The following are the suggestions for basic drinks:

> 1 At least two corkscrews – somebody always tends to walk away with one! – and preferably the corkscrews should be of different types (*see page* 144). A visit to any bar equipment counter, either in a merchant's or at the drinks department of a store will give you a choice of several types of corkscrew.

> 2 You will also need several napkins or thick, plain tissues. These are for wiping the tops of bottles when you open them, and they should not, of course, have been used for anything else which may have given them a scent or smell. Extra strong, thick tissues can substitute if you have no old plain linen napkins.

> 3 You will need a penknife for cutting metal capsules which fit over the cork, and also for dealing with the plastic capsules which are now used for certain inexpensive wines. The type of corkscrew described on page 144, with a brace to it, usually has a penknife attached. Have the knife in any event at hand or else you may break your nails.

4 You also need a bottle opener or lever to remove the tops of bottles of tonics and soda water, and something to pierce the tops of cans of fruit juice which you may require for making mixed drinks.

5 A stopper which can be used for keeping the sparkle in sparkling wines after the cork has come out is useful in even the smallest cellar and you may also have a pair of Champagne nippers which enable the head of the cork to be gripped while the bottle is turned. Both of these are available at shops supplying bar accessories, as well as in the smarter stores, although it is worth pointing out that sometimes the price in the drinks department of a smart store is very much higher than it would be for the same article in an ordinary equipment shop. For decanting, you need either a candle in a fairly firm-standing candle-stick, or a bicycle lamp or similar battery-operated light. A wine cradle or basket may be useful for this (*see pages* 152–154).

6 If you are likely to serve a lot of mixed drinks, then you should have among your ordinary glassware a cocktail shaker and a martini jug, which is an enormous glass with a pinched-in lip to hold back the ice when you pour the drinks after stirring the ingredients together. A long-handled mixing spoon, a barman's knife for cutting slivers of lemon peel, and an ice-bowl are all useful, although perhaps not essential. An ice-bucket is useful if you serve a lot of white wines and your refrigerator is some distance from your dining room, but if you only buy one bucket (an ordinary domestic bowl or bucket is a perfectly adequate although perhaps inelegant substitute), then choose a tall one, which will be referred to as a 'Hock bucket'; this will serve for the long-necked bottles of German and Alsatian white wines, as well as Champagne, but the usual Champagne bucket is too shallow to chill these elongated bottles satisfactorily.

Opening bottles

It is often taken for granted that it is easy to open a bottle. So it is – when everything goes right. If you open the bottle correctly, then there is less likelihood of anything going wrong, but accidents can still happen. The first thing you need is a good corkscrew, and this is not as easy to find as might be supposed, because there are a surprising number of inefficient corkscrews on sale. There are also a number of devices which augment the ordinary corkscrew and make drawing a cork very much easier, but there are still certain things to look out for.

The ideal corkscrew This should be long enough to go right through a long cork – such as might be in a bottle of vintage port or a classed growth claret – and come out the other end. A lot of corkscrews are much too short. The ideal corkscrew is made of a twirl of metal that is rounded, not sharp, so that this spiral goes into the cork and holds it, instead of cutting through it, which a sharp-edge spiral will do, resulting in the corkscrew often being simply drawn straight back through a shattered cork. The ideal corkscrew has a spiral that one can look up, like looking up the coil of a spiral staircase, and it does not end in a point but goes round at the end – a point again simply pierces the cork and cannot possibly gain any purchase on it should it be hard to pull. One of the best for most purposes is the one known as the butterfly, which is a metal or box-wood cylinder that fits over the top of the bottle and with one spiral that is then inserted through the cork; when this is fully inserted, the second 'bow' on the corkscrew is turned and this lifts out the cork easily. There is also an admirable device which works in much the same way by means of two levers. Another type of corkscrew with a trellis attached pulls out the cork quite easily, with the bottle-neck being firmly held with one part of the device, and there are also double-spiralled corkscrews which hold the cork particularly tightly.

You can also buy two-pronged cork extractors, consisting of two pieces of metal of uneven length, which are inserted at either side of a cork, the extractor is given a turn and the cork can then be lifted out of the bottle without being pierced – something very useful if the cork is fragile, as may occur with an old wine. This type is known as a 'butler's friend' because its use meant that it was possible to extract wine from a bottle and then replace the cork, filling up the bottle with something else. The type of corkscrew in use in many bars and by many wine waiters is one that has a brace to hold it against the lip of the bottle while the cork is levered out.

Whichever type you choose, make sure that the spiral is continuous and also that the edge of the screw itself is rounded and not sharp, as this also can simply cut the cork and will not grip it.

Drawing the cork Whichever type of corkscrew or bottle opener is used, there is a simple routine which will facilitate the drawing of a cork for even the hesitant and weak-wristed. First, remove the capsule which covers the cork in the bottle. This can be done by cutting it off just around the top of the neck of the bottle, the cut being made with a penknife, and going right around and under the flange at the very top of the neck. This is important, because any wine poured over a piece of the metal capsule can be tainted with the taste of this. Or you can simply remove the whole of the capsule. This is not elegant, and the smart wine waiter will not do it, but frankly, with a fairly ordinary sort of wine, it doesn't matter in the slightest and it means that you can see exactly what you are doing about drawing the cork or, when you are decanting, you

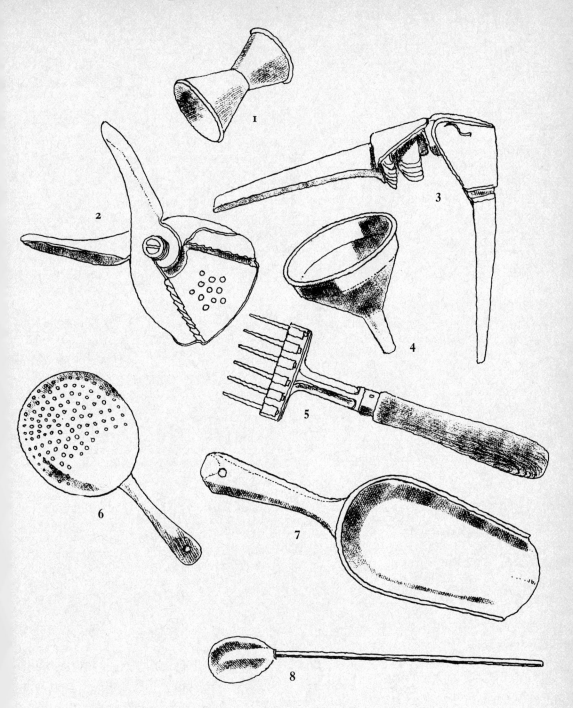

Useful items of bar and cellar equipment: 1 Double-ended measure;
2 and 3 Citrus fruit squeezers; 4 Funnel; 5 Ice chipper; 6 Strainer; 7 Ice
shovel; 8 Mixing spoon.

have a clear view of the wine in the neck of the bottle. So don't be hesitant about doing this if you wish.

Once you have removed the capsule or top part of it, wipe the top of the cork and the surrounding piece of neck with a clean cloth. A surprising amount of dirt will come off and, if you did not remove this, it might remain on the sides of the bottle and get into the wine as this was poured. Then insert the corkscrew or whichever cork extractor is being used. Do this gently and slowly – don't answer the telephone or attend to anyone else while you are opening a bottle: wrap a clean cloth around the bottle so that, as you hold it, your hand is protected from any glass that might cut you should the bottle split – nowadays this is very unlikely, but it can happen, and obviously an accident of this kind could be very unpleasant. Insert the corkscrew slowly right through the cork. Then start to pull, steadily, without jerking. If the cork is tightly wedged in the bottle, then put the bottle on the floor and, with one hand holding the bottle, push downwards, while at the same time pulling upwards with the corkscrew; this combined pushing and pulling usually extracts the most stubborn cork.

When the cork has come out, remove it from the corkscrew (you may need it to re-stopper the bottle temporarily, and it should always be available for inspection by those who find it of interest.). Wipe the neck of the bottle again, because there may be some fragments of cork clinging to it, and there may be some more dirt inside it. Then the wine is ready to be poured, either directly into the glasses or into a decanter.

Coping with a broken cork

If the cork breaks off half-way, then there are two choices of action: you can either remove the piece of the cork attached to the corkscrew, re-insert the screw and very gently try to extract the remaining piece, or, if this is impossible, you can push the piece of cork down into the bottle and pour the wine past it, into a carafe or jug, even if you hadn't previously thought of decanting it. If the cork has crumbled badly, then there will be bits in the wine anyway (this is not the same as the wine being 'corked'), and you will probably have to filter the wine through either a perfectly clean plastic filter or a piece of clean handkerchief, into some suitable receptacle anyway. No one wants to drink a wine that is full of bits. If you are doubtful about being able to pull out any cork, then use a perfectly ordinary corkscrew, but insert it diagonally, instead of through the middle of the cork; this can give extra purchase on the cork, if you then pull it strongly and steadily.

Opening sparkling wines

This again is not difficult, but the procedure is different from the opening of still wines and quite different from what is often seen when people try to show off with a bottle of Champagne.

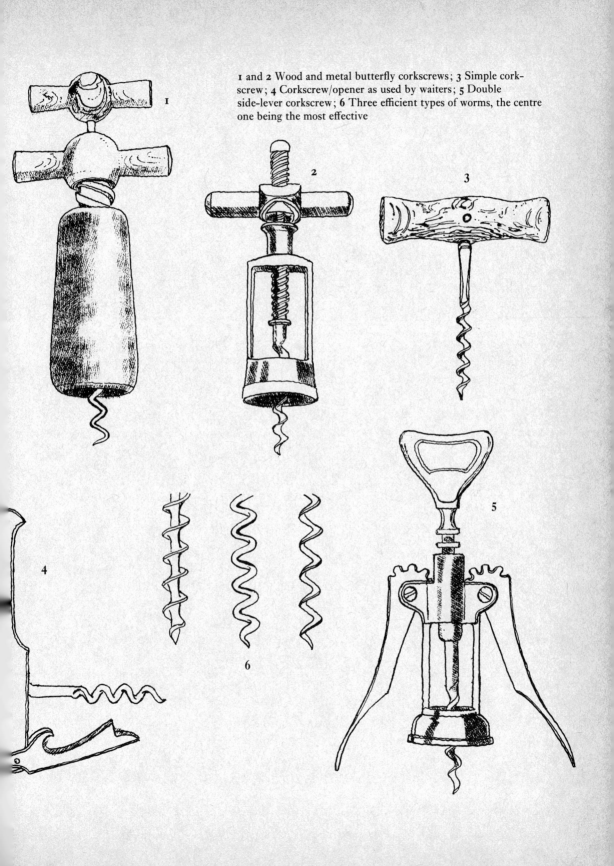

1 and 2 Wood and metal butterfly corkscrews; 3 Simple corkscrew; 4 Corkscrew/opener as used by waiters; 5 Double side-lever corkscrew; 6 Three efficient types of worms, the centre one being the most effective

Again, the bottle should always be held in one hand by a cloth – quite apart from the remote possibility of the bottle splitting, the cloth is useful if the wine is 'lively' and surges down the side of the bottle, should you be unlucky and not get the cork out in the ideal way. Then, holding on to the top of the cork with the other hand, remove the wire muzzle that holds this cork down onto the bottle neck. You start by untwining the muzzle at the point where there is a loop and generally it is quite easy to find this and unwind it. Hold the cork down meanwhile, because sometimes, as soon as the muzzle is lifted, the cork rushes out of the bottle because of the force of the wine behind it. If, however, it does not rise, get rid of the muzzle and, still holding on to the cork, *turn the bottle while keeping the cork firmly in position.* If you turn the cork and not the bottle, you risk breaking off the mushroom at the top of the cork, and then you really will have trouble! Turn the bottle gradually, and you will usually feel the cork begin to rise; do not, at this stage, have the bottle pointing in the direction of anything or anyone that might be hurt by the cork should it fly. Go on easing it out and, when it emerges, it should do so with a very discreet pop, not a vulgar loud noise, and you should have a glass by the bottle into which the wine can immediately be poured. In this way nothing and no one risk injury, not a drop of the wine is wasted, and the whole procedure is both elegant and dignified.

However, all sorts of things can interfere with this ideal procedure. If you have recently shaken the bottle of wine about, perhaps in the boot of a car, a shopping basket, or it is simply a young and lively wine, then there will be tremendous pressure behind the cork and you may not be able to control it once you have got the muzzle off. Remember to incline the bottle at an angle of 45°, which will lessen the pressure slightly. Hang on to both cork and bottle tightly, and put the top of the cloth with which you are holding the bottle right over the top of the cork, which will guard against the cork flying and also blot up any wine that spills. If you are doing this on a picnic, then it is probably not bad advice to suggest putting the palm of your hand immediately over the top of the open bottle as the wine foams up – the slight grease on your palm will check the overflowing wine, just as the butter on the side of a soufflé dish will prevent the soufflé from overflowing – this is perhaps something not to do alongside a dinner table, but it is a practical hint nevertheless.

Problem corks   Suppose you can't get the cork out? It does happen, especially if you have left the wine too long in the refrigerator. It should never be kept there overnight, and, of course, should not be forgotten in the freezer, when all that will result is that you will have an iced wine lolly, which will never be quite the same as a drink again. Champagne nippers can be used; they grip the top of the mushroom-shaped cork, so that you can ease this upwards while you turn the bottle. You can also lever the cork upwards slightly with the pressure of your thumb. But, in fact, the safest way of all and the quickest is to run the hot water tap for a few seconds onto the neck of any bottle of sparkling wine where the cork is sticking. Keep your hand firmly on the cork meanwhile; the heat will increase the pressure behind the cork and you will almost immediately feel it begin to rise, so that you can let it out, controlling its progress, and pour the wine.

If by mischance the top of the cork does break off, and you are unable to get it out by the application of hot water as previously described, then you must pierce the cork with a skewer or very thick needle, so as to release some of the gas behind it; then – and only then – you can use a corkscrew in the ordinary way, but it is essential not to do this before you have released some of the pressure, else you risk the cork coming out with such violence that you may hurt yourself.

Re-corking bottles

It is impossible to put back the cork into a bottle of sparkling wine once it has come out, but there are stoppers available which fasten under the flange at the top of the bottle neck and, by sealing the bottle, retain the sparkle in the wine even if it is left overnight or for about 24 hours. Should you not have one of these and there is need to seal up any sparkling wine remaining in the bottle, then cut a wedge-shaped piece out of the original cork, force this back into the neck of the bottle and tie it down firmly with string, so that it is held under the flange at the top of the neck. If you merely insert an ordinary cork, the gas will build up behind it and the cork will eventually come out again.

With still wines, it is usually fairly simple to re-insert the cork into the bottle. If you drive it down with force, however, you may have to use the corkscrew once more to get it out. If the end of the cork expands after it has been extracted it may be difficult to put it back, and sometimes people are tempted to put the cork in upside down, but this is unwise, as the outer end of the cork may be dirty from the top of the capsule and, with a cork for fine wines, the end which is destined to be in contact with the wine is the superior section of the cork.

If you can't get the cork back in the same condition that you extracted it, then, with a sharp knife, cut a small portion cleanly off either end and re-insert it; the cork, having been cut, will be clean. As air in the bottle will cause the wine to oxidize or deteriorate, it is obvious that the more air there is in the bottle, the quicker the wine will decline. So if you have taken more than half the contents of the bottle out and then wish to re-seal the wine, it is advisable to decant this remaining wine into a smaller bottle if you have one – say a half. The amount of air in this container will be small and the wine will be kept in better condition. Of course, if there is a deposit in the bottle, you must be careful not to pour this into the half bottle as well.

Slightly sparkling or *pétillant* wines will not retain their sparkle if the bottles are left open with the contents unfinished. They, like fully sparkling wines, can still be pleasant drinks if the gas is allowed to escape from the wine, so that you should merely seal the bottle up and put it into a cool place.

Decanting

There are two reasons why some wines benefit by being decanted – although most people would think that there was only one, namely, to pour the wine off any deposit which may be in the bottle. This is true, but certain red wines also benefit by being 'aired' as the action of the atmosphere on them causes them to expand as it were, and give off their beautiful smell and develop their delicious flavour. These things are what you pay for, so it is worth while making sure that, by the correct handling of wines, you are going to enjoy what they have to give.

Deposit in a wine – red or white – is usually the sign of a fine wine, and has formed during a period of time in which the wine has been undergoing maturation in bottle. If the bottle has been kept lying down, then this deposit will be on the underside, towards the base, and when the bottle is stood up for any length of time the deposit will settle in the bottom of the bottle. It spoils the appearance of a fine wine to have a drink in the glass that is cloudy and the taste of the deposit can also be unpleasant, so that the process of decanting is simply to pour the clear bright wine off this deposit.

The process of aeration, which is the second reason for decanting, is so that certain wines which may be, as it were, shy and hesitant to display their charm when they are simply poured from a bottle, may, by contact with the air, delight the drinker. Because contact with the air brings on the age of a wine, it is helpful to a very young wine, which may not yet be at its peak for drinking, to subject it to airing in this way, as well as for a wine that may be of reserved character, needing time to get used to the atmosphere. This is why it is important to consider the type of wine which you are going to decant, because some wines can benefit by several hours airing, others, when they are exposed to the air, will decline rather rapidly. Only experience can give you an exact idea of what to do, but the person from whom you bought your wine should be able to advise if you are in doubt.

When to decant One fairly sound maxim is 'an old wine deserves decanting, a young wine needs it', and when you are wondering about the length of time that a red wine should be aired, then adopt the rule-of-thumb habit of giving any wine a minimum of one hour in the decanter ahead of the time that it is to be served (unless you are handling a wine 20–30 years old, when you probably know what you are doing anyway).

If you are deliberately opening a bottle of a wine that you know will be really too young to drink and want to help it on, you can decant it two or three hours ahead of time. Suppose you have a good ordinary wine, which you think is nevertheless a little harsh in style – try opening this and decanting it, even into a carafe or jug, which you then cover lightly with a tissue or cloth, three to four hours ahead of the time you want to drink it. See then whether you enjoy it more – you probably will.

In fact, the whole process of decanting depends on what you enjoy: try, one day when you have cause to open two bottles of wine, to decant one an hour or a little more ahead of time, and then simply draw the cork of the other one and, with two glasses in front of you, decide which you prefer. This will enable you to judge what to do in the future.

How to decant   Decanting is comparatively simple, but it is something that cannot be undertaken if you are likely to be interrupted, so don't answer the telephone, the doorbell, attend to the children or interrupt the process for *anything* short of a major and immediate disaster. You need nothing by way of equipment, apart from a corkscrew, a knife to cut the capsule off the top of the bottle, a cloth with which to hold the bottle, the decanter, carafe or jug into which the wine is to be poured and – the only special piece of equipment –

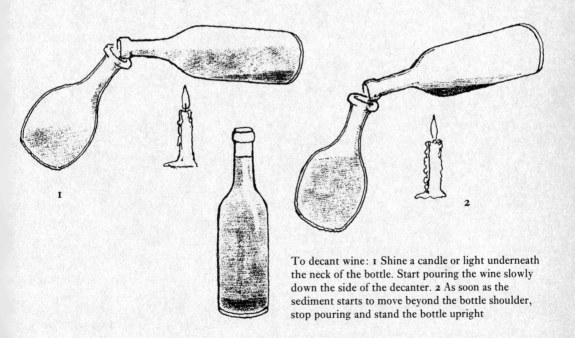

To decant wine: 1 Shine a candle or light underneath the neck of the bottle. Start pouring the wine slowly down the side of the decanter. 2 As soon as the sediment starts to move beyond the bottle shoulder, stop pouring and stand the bottle upright

some form of light which can shine behind or underneath the neck of the bottle. You can use a candle for this, or else a torch, bicycle lamp or small reading lamp with a bright bulb. The only important thing is that the source of illumination should be adequate so that you can see, as you pour the wine from bottle to decanter, when the deposit in the wine begins to move up the bottle, at which point you must stop pouring.

Draw the cork of the bottle (*see page* 144). Light the candle or switch on the torch or lamp. You are going to hold the decanter with one hand and the bottle with another, so it depends whether you are right- or left-handed as to which way round you do this. After you have wiped the neck of the bottle, begin to pour the wine slowly into the clean decanter, ideally allowing it to run down the side of the decanter and not splash directly into the middle of this, which may aerate the wine too much. Pour slowly and steadily, being careful not to jerk the bottle or tip it up and down, which action will churn up any deposit and make the wine muddy. Watch, meanwhile, by means of the light, where the deposit in the bottle is – you will see it begin to move from the base of the bottle up into the body, and from there into the neck. As soon as it passes the shoulder of the bottle, put the bottle upright again gently, and set it down.

If you wish to try the wine at this stage, then, with the bottle still inclined at the same angle as that which you have been holding it to pour into the decanter, pour a little of the remaining still bright or clear wine into a nearby glass. You can use this for tasting, and even if a little deposit has got into it you will not spoil the contents of the decanter, which you will by now have set down and stoppered or covered.

It is the steady pouring which is important, for if you tilt the decanter up and down in any way this will churn the wine up in the bottle and the deposit will muddy the wine.

The wine cradle If you have understood the procedure of decanting, you will see exactly how and why the wine cradle should be used – and how it should not. The cradle, which holds the bottle of wine at an angle, is so that, when a bottle is taken from the bin in which it has been lying on its side, it need not be stood upright at all; instead, still held in the cradle, it can be opened and the wine gradually poured into the decanter, always inclined at the same angle, so that the deposit cannot join the bright wine which is flowing into the decanter. *This is the only part that the wine cradle has to play.* Its use on the dining table is a piece of pure wine chi-chi, because it is not only quite unnecessary to serve many wines in this way – for example, good everyday wines, which throw no deposit at all and which can perfectly well be served with the bottle set down again in an upright position – or, if it should be used for wine that has any sort of deposit in the bottle, the tipping up and down action will simply make the wine that is poured into the glasses of the diners resemble soup by the time it has been repeated even twice.

Wine waiters will use cradles; managements say that customers require it, and customers in their own homes like the 'atmosphere' they suppose to be created by the cradle. But, in fact, a cradle or anything that holds a bottle inclined has no place whatsoever on the dining table or sideboard of the host or hostess who has taken the trouble previously to prepare a bottle by standing it up or by decanting it. Even if, at the very last minute, you draw a bottle from your bin or bottle rack, the cradle should be used away from the dining table. Some people are silly enough to serve anything, including young white wines as well as everyday reds, from a cradle, but this is as much a piece of mid-20th century chi-chi as it would be, in the pseudo 'historic' feasts that are currently rather fashionable, for chamber pots to be kept in the sideboard or guests to relieve themselves in corners of the dining room.

Should you at very short notice have occasion to serve a wine that has thrown a big deposit, then either put it in the cradle or, keeping it inclined, preferably propped up at the same angle at which it has lain, draw the cork and pour out the wine into the glasses all at the same time, merely gradually inclining the bottle a little more. This process, as you will see if you can reflect on what has been said, will prevent the tilting up and down of the bottle which churns up the deposit in the base; you will have several glassfuls

1 Hold the wine cradle firmly with one hand while drawing the cork carefully with the other. **2** Slowly pour the wine into the decanter, keeping the bottle, as far as possible, at the same angle it was at when opened

of wine that are bright and limpid, of a beautiful colour and unclouded, the sediment, if any, remaining in the bottle – which wine you can use up in cooking.

Pouring wine   To pour wine from a bottle into a glass is a simple enough procedure, yet it is not often that people do it in what is the correct and most convenient way: hold the bottle or decanter firmly, with your hand around the body of the bottle, fingers spread out to steady it. Direct the wine into the centre of the wine glass and stop pouring when this is half or, at most, two-thirds full. If you then turn the bottle very slightly and lift it at the same time, there will be no drip either into the glass or on the table cloth; it is easy to practice this and, if you are right-handed, make this slight turn – about a quarter turn – clockwise. Unless you are absolutely sure that there is no speck of sediment in the bottom of the bottle or decanter, do not tip this upside down over the glass when you come to the end of the wine – it is not very elegant to be seen shaking the very last drop out of the bottle, and you may get some deposit in even the most carefully-handled bottle if you do this.

Chapter 8 *The Social Side of Drinking*

Wine parties

Wine parties are a fairly recent but very popular form of entertainment. Some people use them as means of raising funds for various charitable purposes, others find them a pleasant variation on the cocktail party, and for many they give interest to what might otherwise be a rather ordinary type of buffet meal.

It is always a good idea for a wine party to have a theme: you may wish to offer a selection of wines from a region with pleasant holiday associations; often, with the co-operation of a wine merchant, you can have a selection of wines that are likely to be novelties to most of your friends. Sometimes it is possible to revive the now rather old-fashioned sherry party by offering two, three or four types of sherry for people to choose and compare, or you can have a comparison of sparkling or *pétillant* wines; a very pretty tasting party, for example, could be built around a complete range of pink wines, each one accompanied by a rose most nearly matching it in colour. If you know the food of a particular wine region, especially one of the areas in which meals are informal rather than formal, such as some of the Mediterranean countries and areas where salads and snack food are the local specialities, then a buffet of this kind, with several of the local wines, can be very pleasant.

As with wine tastings, it is always a good idea to limit the number of wines you serve at such parties, and preferably to restrict them to table wines, with the possible exception of the selection of sherries previously mentioned. You can offer white and tawny port or a selection of Madeiras, if you like, but if you are also going to feed people, then a table wine or a selection of table wines is more or less essential. Ideally, too, have some kind of introductory drink – this is where you can include your sherry or fortified wine – before people taste the selection of other wines; and try, with the table wines, to arrange them in the order in which they will taste most enjoyable: white before red, dry before sweet and, unless the prices are all about the same, the cheaper ones before the more expensive ones. For preference, choose your wines within the same price range, however, because then, if people do go back and help themselves when they are eating, you will be sure that supplies will not run out unevenly, as may happen when everyone drinks the expensive wines first.

If you are able to arrange such a wine party with the co-operation of a wine merchant, then quite often the merchant will have maps or photographs of the wine regions concerned, or may be able to give you any other information about the wines, which can add to the general interest. It is worth while planning the mechanics of such an event in detail, so that it does not become a mere free-for-all, but is a party with a plan.

People should be given a single glass, which they must be told to keep, and, if the numbers are large, and especially if you are doing this to make money, there should be helpers to pour the wines, so that supplies are regulated and no one gets more than a fair share at a time. Space out the bottles, so that people do not jostle each other and risk upsetting the wines, and ideally have the food apart from the drinks, so that this too does not complicate service or self-service.

In order to be able to judge quantities involved, you should count on getting about 16 tasting samples out of each bottle, if these are poured; at a professional tasting, a skilled pourer can eke out the contents of a bottle to 20 samples, but if people are paying for a ticket, then they will probably want a little more than this. In addition to arranging spittoons, which can be the professional sort, or simply cartons or wooden cases filled with sawdust or sand, there should be bottles fitted with funnels in which the drainings of any tasting samples may be poured when people have finished. Ideally, try and borrow magnums from someone for this, because this means that they will not be confused with bottles actually included in the tasting.

It can also be helpful to have piles of white paper napkins for people to wipe their fingers, and, of course, the cloth with which the tasting table is covered should also be white – white paper will do instead of cloth. If you are having printed or duplicated tasting sheets, give plenty of space for people to jot down their remarks and, should you be organizing a tasting in conjunction with a wine merchant, it is a courtesy to give some indication as to prices of the wines offered at the tasting and where they may be obtained.

Suggestions for the choice of wine for tasting

Study tastings: Compare and discuss several examples, from different sources of supply, of any of the following wines:

1 Fino sherries
2 Wines made like sherry from other countries than Spain

3 Three or four ports of the same vintage but from different port shippers

4 Three or four Champagnes of the same vintage from different Champagne houses

5 A progression of red Burgundy or Bordeaux wines from either the same vintages but different areas, or the same area and vineyards, but a wider range of vintages

6 A comparison of wines of approximately the same age made from a single grape variety, chosen from widely different wine regions; for example the Cabernet or Riesling grape from California, South Africa, Australia and any of the European vineyards.

These are only general suggestions, but anyone taking part in such tastings should ideally have already learnt a little about wine and be able to discuss the tasting samples with some knowledge, even gained only by reading about the wines concerned.

Wine parties:
1 A selection of table wines, red and white, from any wine region associated with holidays, such as the Loire valley, Greece, Cyprus, Spain, and North Portugal

2 A range of Italian wines, sparkling and still – ideally, such a range would come from one single source of supply, as the different shippers have individual styles of the different wines and it is better to be as consistent as possible

3 A selection of the sparkling wines of the world other than those made by the Champagne process. Sparkling wines made by the Champagne process but not including Champagne could be an alternative

4 A tasting of rosé wines from all over the world

5 A tasting of pairs of wines, each made from the same grape, but one coming from a classic European vineyard and the other from somewhere else – for example, Alsatian and Hungarian Riesling, Loire and Californian Chenin Blanc, the Cabernet Franc of Chinon with the same grape from Australia, the Sauvignon Blanc of Bordeaux with the same wine from a Californian vineyard, and so on

6 It should also be possible to show a complete range of a region's wines, such as that of Tuscany in Italy, the Rhône valley in France.

White or rosé wines are usually more suited to this type of general party, but, if you also offer rather simple food, you might also show three or four types of Beaujolais or southern Burgundy, bourgeois clarets, or the red wines of the Rhône. Variations on this kind of theme are virtually endless.

How much to allow

The fear of running out of drink before the end of a party is somehow worse than fearing that there will not be enough food to go round. But it is quite easy to calculate how much you are likely to need and, as far as wines for a party are concerned, it is worth knowing that most sources of supply will let you have bottles on a sale or return basis, which means that, if you do not open the bottle, they will take it back and refund your money. Bottles are fairly standard in size and experience has shown that there is not much variation as to the amount that people will drink in normal circumstances, so that you can easily calculate how much you should allow.

The standard wine bottle holds 75 centilitres, although, of course, there may be a little air under the cork, so that the actual liquid content is slightly less. You should never complain about this, unless the ullage, as this space is called, is serious, but in a very fine old wine the amount of air under the cork may be more than for an everyday wine and, if the wine is all right, there is no cause for complaint about this. A few wine bottles only hold about 70 centilitres, and litre bottles are being increasingly used for inexpensive wines, which are also now being put up in even larger sizes.

Remember that, with quality wines, a half bottle will mature faster than a bottle, and a bottle faster than a magnum (equivalent to two bottles), although the magnum is probably the ideal size for the finest wines, especially the great clarets and vintage Champagne so that, as far as vintage wines are concerned, you should remember that the larger the size the slower the wine will take to reach its peak drinking period. Sometimes people ask why more wines are not bottled in half bottles, but as it costs nearly as much to 'package' the wine in a half bottle as in a whole bottle, and virtually as much to handle it, it is obvious that the half-bottle size is not really economical. Anyway, as you will have noted, it is perfectly easy, with most wines, to cork up the bottle if you do not finish it at a sitting, or decant it into a half bottle to keep it in good condition for another meal.

Sizes of helpings

The following quantities are assessed on the assumption that you will be using a reasonably-sized glass (not less than $5\frac{1}{2}$ fl. oz and possibly up to about 8 fl. oz) and that you are only filling each half-way or two-thirds up.

Still table wines: Allow seven to eight helpings per bottle with the usual 75 cl. wine bottle. With certain very fine red wines, such as clarets and red Burgundy, there may be a deposit in the bottom of the bottle, and then you should allow fewer servings per bottle, as the dregs can be saved for use in cooking or making into vinegar.

Champagne and sparkling wines: Allow about six glasses to the bottle, as the bottles for this type of wine have to be slightly thicker and, therefore, there is a little less wine inside. If for any reason you have simply got to use the shallow Champagne saucer glass, or have the very tall narrow flute glasses, which are extremely elegant for this type of wine, then you will probably get more helpings out of the bottle.

Sherry, port and Madeira: Allow about 12 helpings per bottle, or 10 if you prefer one generous helping to two rounds before a meal. If you get any more than this out, then frankly your glasses are too small!

Vermouth and apéritifs in general: About 10 to 12 helpings per bottle may be allowed if you are drinking these wines neat, but obviously if you are making them into long drinks with soda or a similar additive and serving them in a tall glass, then you may be able to count on twice the number of helpings. Obviously, if you like your spirit-based mixed drinks very 'dry' indeed, then a bottle of vermouth such as one might have for making dry martinis could do for 25 to 30 drinks. But this is something that only experience can teach you and most people who mix their own cocktails have highly individual ideas as to quantities and proportions, so it is difficult to generalize here.

Gin, whisky, brandy, rum, vodka: The bar measure calculates 25 helpings per bottle but, of course, this quantity will depend greatly on whether people are making their drinks short or long, or whether they intend to drink the spirits neat. Some people, too, prefer one double helping to two singles, and if you are serving malt whisky or liqueur brandy after a meal with no diluting agent at all, then people will probably prefer a slightly larger helping than if they were going to have the same spirit with water or a similar mix. This again is something that can only be learnt about by experience, and the type of helping that people prefer is often greatly affected by the time of day and the circumstances in which they drink – for example, a leisurely drink late at night is quite a different thing from one taken at the end of lunch on a working day, or as a refresher early in the evening. Miniatures of spirits, such as are often sold on aeroplanes or in theatre bars, usually provide one single, but quarter bottles of spirits will give you four to six reasonable helpings.

Liqueurs: The bar measure is 32 helpings per bottle, but this also must obviously be a matter of personal choice, conditioned likewise by whether you are going to serve these drinks with any additional mineral water, use them in a mixed drink, or pour them over ice; remember, the ice will dilute the drink, so it is only fair to be a little more generous with a helping when poured in this way. A miniature of a liqueur usually provides for two small portions or one generous measure.

It is embarrassing to guests and even more so to hosts and hostesses if there is an obvious measuring out of wine, perhaps with a sudden sortie to draw the cork of another half bottle! Equally, it is badly proportioned hospitality if you give your guests several strong spirit-based cocktails before a meal and a mere scant glass of wine with the food. Avoid this kind of thing by remembering the sound music hall precept – always leave them wanting more. In other words, be generous with your hospitality throughout (this does not mean being unnecessarily lavish) but make sure that, while no one is pressed to drink more than they wish, a reasonable amount is provided for all so that, at the end of the entertainment, guests will feel that they want to repeat the experience some time, instead of merely rushing home or to the nearest pub to give themselves a reviving drink and vow that they won't visit you again! Build your drinks to a satisfactory climax and then stop.

If you have allowed a reasonable amount per head, then there is no need to open anything more at the last moment; in fact this is nearly always a mistake, especially with wines that accompany food, because at best the wine is unlikely to be at the correct temperature and, by being chosen so suddenly, it may be wholly out of keeping with the rest of the food and drinks.

People vary tremendously in the amount that they like to drink. This is only a problem, however, with strangers, and you will usually find that you tend to drink about the same amount as your friends, so that, if you go by what you yourself would prefer, this is as safe a guide as any with all but a very large and mixed party. Here anyway are some general ideas about quantities, worked out as the result of experience and consultation with a number of caterers.

How much when? People tend to drink more in the evening than during the day, less if they can sit down during a party than if they have to stand up all the time. As far as spirits are concerned, especially with regard to short drinks, they may drink more cocktails and similar spirit-based drinks overall in the winter than the summer.

If you are serving long drinks, such as any type of cup or something based on a spirit with a lot of soda, ginger ale or tonic added to it, people will probably drink more of these at a general drinks party in hot weather simply because they want to quench their thirst; the same applies if you are giving a party in a centrally-heated house or flat with the temperature set rather high.

As people travel so much and mix so widely today, never be surprised at peoples' drinking habits. For example, in many European countries, even in some of the wine regions, you may not be offered an apéritif before a meal at all, but go into dinner or lunch within a few minutes of assembling.

PLATE 8: *A breathtaking view of Portugal's mountainous Douro valley; port can only come from grapes grown in these steeply-terraced vineyards.*

PLATE 9: *Harvesters, in the time-honoured way, spread out grapes on mats of esparto grass to dry partially before they are pressed to make sherry.*

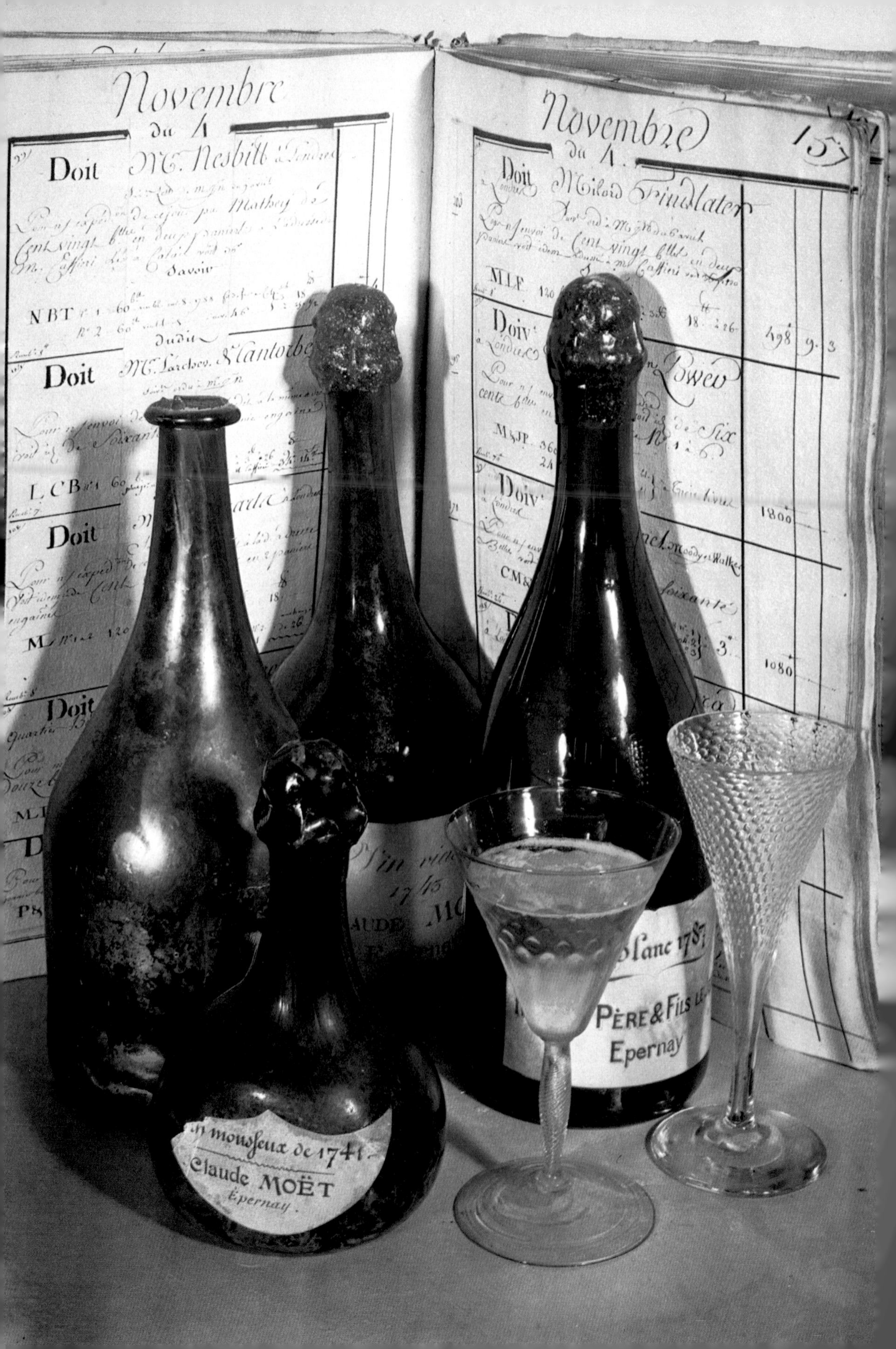

In Britain it is generally accepted as normal to offer, even if not to accept, two drinks before a meal per head, but in some homes one is regarded as quite sufficient.

Sometimes women who do not work outside their homes are astonished at the amount of drink put away, apparently without any effect, by others to whom a drink or two during the working day and again during the evening is routine. In some circles it would, until comparatively recently, have been almost shocking for a teenager to ask for a whisky and soda or gin and tonic at a family party; nowadays this is not necessarily something to criticize because, after all, if they are accustomed to drinking in moderation with their parents, they will probably learn something about what they like and how much they can take with enjoyment. People who are tired may really want a much stronger single drink than you might have thought of giving them – if in doubt, ask them to mix their own. Here, then, are some generalizations that may prove helpful:

If people drop in for drinks, calculate on offering them two drinks minimum, although many people will possibly only accept a single helping. If you choose to offer them a table wine on such an occasion, then unless you have a number of visitors the emptying of the bottle is an indication that no more will be served and you will not be thought inhospitable by anyone.

For drinks before a meal, allow two drinks per head, but if you serve a sparkling wine, you may find that one generous glassful is enough for certain guests. It is to be assumed that they will be drinking another wine with their meal after all.

If the meal is delayed for any reason, then you may at least offer more drinks, whether or not people accept them.

For drinks after a meal, allow one and a half or two glasses of port, a dessert wine, or a similar helping of brandy, but you will usually find that, should you offer a liqueur, guests will only take a single helping of this. Of course, if people do arrive just for coffee and drinks, as is becoming increasingly popular, you should ideally be prepared to offer them a little more to drink than if they had been dining with you.

The drinks party: People tend to come and go at this type of party, but it is probably fair to allow from two to two and a half hours' drinking time. If you intend guests to stay for a longer period, then you should certainly increase the overall allowance of drinks, but, in addition, be sure to provide some food of a more substantial nature than simply nuts, biscuits, olives and similar cocktail nibbles. People tend to drink a little more if only wine is offered, even if this is Champagne, and you will be safe if you allow for five or six wine helpings per head in a two-hour drinks party, or three to five

PLATE 10: Highly-prized legacies of the past are these very old Champagne bottles, together with an old account book of the Champagne house of Moët et Chandon. The bottle dated 1741 is the oldest unopened bottle of Champagne in existence

of sherry or a spirit-based drink in the same time. Of course, some people will only have one or two drinks and others much more, but this is a working average.

Champagne party: If you serve Champagne or a quality sparkling wine exclusively throughout a party, then a reasonable allowance is two-thirds of a bottle per head for adults accustomed to enjoying wine, especially if the party takes place in the evening. If it is a morning party, and you have a very mixed gathering – perhaps for some family celebration, with both older and some very young guests – then you can probably manage on half a bottle per head. If you make a sparkling wine the basis for a mixed drink, perhaps combining it with orange juice for Buck's Fizz, or putting one bottle of sparkling wine to two of still for Cold Duck, then allow slightly more for drinks all round.

Weddings: The standard allowance to calculate at a wedding is half a bottle of sparkling wine or Champagne per head – or rather per adult head. If the wedding reception goes on for some time, however, and there is no formal meal served, then it is as well to have extra supplies in case they are needed; if you make your plans with the caterers in advance, there is no problem about this, but it is wise to be definite that only one person – father or mother of the bride or whoever is responsible for the wedding – can give the authority to open any more bottles once the permitted quantity has been served. If you are serving only a sparkling wine at the moment of toasting the bridal pair, then of course a single drink all round is all that is needed, as presumably you will offer other drinks beforehand.

Buffet parties: If people are standing up throughout the entire party, they will tend to drink more and eat less than if they are able to sit down. Also, if you have people to pour the wines or can yourself circulate with bottles, then consumption will be slightly reduced, although it is often far easier to put the bottles on the buffet table or on the small tables at which people may sit and simply let them help themselves.

If you are serving any type of short drink whether cocktails or sherry before the actual buffet, and certainly if you are offering spirits to drink afterwards, then your allowances of wine per head can be slightly reduced. Should you want to offer some kind of short drink or apéritif, then allow two or, ideally, three of such drinks per head, plus half a bottle of wine with the food. But if you are serving wine throughout, then it is prudent to allow a bottle per head for the whole party.

You may prefer to serve only a single type of wine with the buffet, but if you do have a choice of, say, red or white, or red or rosé, then you usually find that, unless you can keep the white or pink wine really cool, people will concentrate on the red and you will run out of this sooner than of the other. In fact, unless you have domestic help or can employ catering staff, it is not usually a good idea to have a choice of several wines for a buffet party unless this is on a fairly small scale. People can always be given a glass of white wine by way of apéritif and stick to this, if they wish, even if you only have red or rosé with the buffet. And, of course, the type of food you serve on such occasions does dictate to some extent the choice of wine, although there are many excellent red and white wines that can interchange as accompaniments to the sort of foods which are popular for these informal parties.

If you are serving sparkling wine throughout a buffet party, then you must allow at least a single bottle per head, as, in the course of an evening and whilst eating, some people anyway will consume as much if not more.

Quantities with meals: For purely social occasions it may be assumed that people may prefer to drink rather less in the middle of the day than at dinner, although for certain business and celebration luncheons, the reverse may be true. Nor should it ever be assumed that men by themselves will drink more than the same number of people at a mixed party – if women, especially women in business, are accustomed to enjoying wine, then they will possibly consume quite as much table wine as the men, although they may go easier on any fortified wines or spirits before and after the meal. Naturally, a party consisting of a number of people not accustomed to drinking wine more than several times a year will not get through as much as those to whom a bottle of wine is a usual accompaniment to many meals. But it is a wise policy always to allow more than just a bare glass per head, even if people are convinced that they will drink no more. Any wine left over need not be wasted and there is something extraordinarily dampening to the spirits if you are, as it were, rationed to the amount you drink; this does not make for a relaxed and friendly atmosphere at the dinner table.

It is true that it is quite difficult to know how much to allow for six people, a fairly usual number for guests, and the situation is further complicated by the fact that, if you serve more than one wine in the course of a meal, people will not always drink more overall. But then, they don't eat the same amount either and therefore hard and fast rules are difficult to establish. Generally, however, a minimum of half a bottle per head is quite reasonable; this provides for three to four helpings each and, in the course of a three-course meal or one that is longer, three glasses of wine is about the least that you can expect people to take, because of course some will want more, although others drink less. If you have been very lavish with your cocktails or served Champagne or a sparkling wine before dinner, then you could make do with two bottles for six people, but three would be better. If you are four to dinner, then one bottle is enough – but only just, and restriction to this single bottle means that the hostess has got to be a very modest drinker and that, ideally, some sort of dessert wine or spirits should be offered after the meal.

If you serve two wines at a meal, one with the first course and the other with what is the principal dish before the sweet, then naturally people tend to take more of the second wine. At a dinner for six people, you could have a single bottle of wine for the opening course and follow it with two of the second wine. With eight to dinner, allow a bottle and a half of the first wine and you can probably manage with two of the second, but it might be safer to have two bottles of the first. If you are in any doubt about peoples' preferences for white or red, then allow some extra of the first bottle if this is a white wine, in addition to the per capita potential consumption, so that if anyone wants to continue drinking this wine they can do so throughout the meal. In fact, with eight people around the table, you could make one bottle of wine go round with the first course, and then not refresh the glasses subsequently at all, but in this instance there ought certainly to be three bottles of the second wine, and four might be wise.

Special wine dinners: Sometimes people like to compare several red wines at a meal and this can be extremely interesting if the diners are students of the subject. If you are going to do this, and if you have only a very limited supply of the wines, having perhaps bought some very special bottles for the occasion, then it is wise to warn people in advance that this sort of drink will be limited anyway, so that they do not toss it off and then ask vainly for more. People have been known to do this with historic and rare wines and finish their helpings while other guests are still discussing the drinks – and then the host may be called on to sacrifice some of a precious wine still remaining to him. If you do plan a special wine dinner of this type, then it is probably advisable to be fairly generous with the first wine, should you later have to limit those that qualify as 'fine and rare'.

And at a very special meal, which may take some hours to eat, and at which the wines will be discussed eagerly as well as the food, it is certainly not extravagant to allow a bottle per head, exclusive of any drinks served before and after the meal; people may exclaim in horror at the idea of allowing so much, but in fact if you take three or four hours over a meal of more than three courses, the actual effect of the alcohol need not be as great as if you drank even a half bottle in a hurry, with very little food by way of blotting paper. But, of course, such occasions are rare and infrequent and anyone planning them will almost certainly get advice from someone experienced in wine.

Big bottles: A curious thing which has been noted by everyone serving wine out of large bottles, whether litres or magnums, is that the wine from such large containers always seems to go further than it would if poured from the equivalent number of bottles! There is no logical explanation for this, but of course a big bottle is always a handsome adjunct to every kind of party; perhaps the sight of the big bottle is so satisfying to the eye that the appetite for its contents is somehow cut down! Of course, should there be any deposit, which involves the wasting of perhaps half a glass of wine out of each standard bottle, then this will be less if all the wine comes out of a single large one.

Wine and children
Many people are horrified at the idea of any alcoholic beverage being given to children, but in fact millions of those who grow up in wine-producing regions appear to have suffered no ill effects from an occasional and moderate helping of wine from an early age. And it is a fact that the system of even the most conscientious and lifelong teetotaller contains a tiny fraction of alcohol. There is also the circumstance that a young person who, from a fairly early age, has seen wine treated as an enjoyable asset to entertaining and a wholly civilized pleasure, is unlikely to over-indulge as soon as he or she can do so. It is, after all, the abuse not the use of the good things in life that is to be condemned. If a child is accustomed to having a few drops of wine, perhaps not more than a teaspoonful, to colour the water it drinks at a special meal, or has a sip of a sparkling wine at a family celebration, then no harm is likely to be done, then or in the future.

The restaurant wine list

Many people admit to being timid about ordering wine in restaurants. But if they have understood this book, they can be sure they know at least as much if not much more than the average wine waiter! As with all shopping, it helps to know a little about the subject, to be firm about what you have to spend and to have formed some ideas about what you like and about what your guests may enjoy. You have to have some friendship with and much confidence in any eating place before you simply say, 'I'll leave it all to you' to either waiter or wine waiter; in general such people tend to prefer customers who express opinions of their own, instead of throwing the responsibility on staff at what may be a hectic time – and the individual waiter concerned may not have had enough special training to give individual service of the kind you probably want. But whether you are simply entertaining a few friends, organizing a meal for business associates, or simply ensuring that you yourself have a reasonable drink with a meal if you are eating out, there are a few simple procedures which will make your task easier.

Ordering in advance
If you are organizing a very special meal in a top restaurant, then it is only sensible to order the wines when you order the food – ideally in advance of

the day. You can then get the opinions of as many authoritative people as possible on the sort of drinks that are likely to be most enjoyable, and can discuss this with the wine waiter (by appointment), being perfectly frank about the details of the entertainment and about how much you want to spend. There is nothing to be hesitant about in saying, 'That is too expensive'; this is far better than if you oblige a poor waiter to eke out a very limited supply of something that you can't really afford anyway. Naturally tell the wine waiter what you are going to eat, mention any wines that you have heard of or previously tried that you think might be suitable, see if he can provide them or similar ones either from his list or from the small store of special bottles that a good restaurant of even moderate size usually has available for customers on such important occasions.

Ordering wines in advance is not only a practice that sets you free to enjoy your own party, but it enables the wine waiter to serve the wines you order to advantage – the white wines correctly chilled, the red wines at room temperature and, if necessary, decanted. To expect him to start doing much of this at a time when he may be rushed off his feet, much less discuss with you in detail the sort of thing that you think you might be likely to order, is not being very considerate – and only an exceptional establishment (although they do exist) will be able to cope with this to your satisfaction.

If you don't order the meal in advance, then you should at least order the wines as soon as you order your food. Again, ideally, this is done while you are having your apéritifs, preferably in the bar or before you go to the table. It is over-optimistic to expect a busy waiter to be able to attend to your wine requirements immediately, should you get into the dining room and sit down before you have even thought of ordering drinks. Sometimes it can be difficult to get the wine list the same time as the menu, but it is both sense to try and insist that you do have it early, and also to make it perfectly clear that you want your wine or wines served *with* your food – not afterwards; if the wine you have ordered with your first course isn't presented as soon as you sit down and the food is served, then, if you can bring yourself to do so, refuse to have the food served until the wine makes its appearance. Polite insistence on this, in a pleasant way, is better than having your white wine with the roast beef and your claret with the pudding!

When you get the list   If you are only going to drink a glass, carafe or half carafe of wine, then you can merely ask if this is available and, possibly, enquire what the wine is, and then let the waiter get on with his job. But if you are studying the list, make sure that the wine waiter (or wine waitress) knows what you are going to eat, and then ask for a suggestion: ideally, the perfect *sommelier* or wine waiter should suggest two wines, one possibly in the expensive category, the other more modest, so that it is up to you to choose. He may also, if he is expert at his job, ask what sort of wines you prefer. But if he cannot make a contribution in this way, then it is up to you to take the initiative.

The wine waiter may play safe and suggest some well-known and widely advertised branded wine that you have previously tried; there is nothing wrong with your ordering this, although it may mark you out as a more discriminating customer if you comment that you do know this drink but that you would like to have something else for a change, so what is of particular interest?

Incidentally, if you are speaking to any type of table staff – waiter, waitress, or wine waiter – bear in mind that they may not speak your language as a native, so make it easy for them to understand what you want: look at them when you speak, smile, at least at the beginning of the conversation, and put your questions and give your orders in as concise a way as possible, without bewildering them and taking up their time with lengthy anecdotes, funny stories, or pointless questions.

It is absolutely useless to ask, 'Is that nice?' about any wine, because you are hardly likely to encounter someone who will reply, 'Actually, I think it reminds me of cough mixture and fizzy lemonade, and the manager, who we think may have been drunk at the time, took it as a job lot off someone who owed us money.' The poor waiter has *got* to say, 'Very nice', or simply agree with you. If, on the other hand, you say that you have ordered a grilled sole and you usually like a Moselle to drink with fish, then it is up to him either to suggest one off his list or, if he has nothing suitable, to recommend perhaps an Alsatian wine or maybe something from the Loire. If you say that you would have preferred to drink claret with your steak, but you don't know any of the wines listed, then he can either recommend one in particular or else, perhaps playing safe, suggest a good Beaujolais if they have one or maybe another red wine.

If you have read that Muscadet is a good partner for shellfish (after all, you've been reading about wine now and you should be able to remember or look up some of the recommendations), then it is up to him to serve you one if he has it, or if not, to try and produce something similar. Be careful, though, if you ask whether a wine is dry or not, for there is such a snobbery about this kind of thing that it has been known for waiters anxious to please to say that full-bodied and almost sweet fine wines were really 'Very dry and light' and a very dry, crisp wine was 'Full – not at all sharp'. If he plays too safe and suggests that, at a table where you and your guests have ordered different dishes, some meat and some fish, you should all drink rosé and you would prefer (as, after reading this book, you probably would) something of more definite style, then *say* so – ask him if he has a white Burgundy good enough to partner this kind of thing? (Again, if you have read the book, you will know!)

Specialized If a restaurant specializes in a specific type of food – Italian, French, Spanish,
restaurants Greek – and especially if the wine waiter comes from the country concerned,
you should certainly ask for his advice. In this way you will often get the
chance to taste wines that are new and interesting to you and which you may
pass by if you play safe. But do accept the fact that the major wine countries
are large and you are hardly likely to get, say, a Sicilian recommending
a Tuscan wine if he can persuade you to try one from his own island;
nor will a Burgundian necessarily have detailed knowledge of the red wines
of Bordeaux – each will try to sell you the wines with which he is familiar
and which he naturally loves.

Wines for Let there be no nonsense whatsoever about 'sweet white wine for the ladies':
women if your guests – of either sex – are unaccustomed to wine drinking, they may
indeed prefer a wine that has a slight softness to it or, if you have chosen a red
wine, something that is fruity rather than too subtle, but, just as all men are
not the same, so all women can be different.

Meat and fish If you are faced with the problem of some people having ordered meat
at once and some fish, then the safe all-round choice is probably a white wine of
medium character, not too dry, but definitely not sweet, with sufficient
assertiveness to partner the meat, yet not so much that a delicate sauce will
be overwhelmed. White Burgundy has the reputation for being the most all-
purpose wine in the world, but in fact most wine regions have a wine that
will fit this description adequately – although again, in most wine regions, the
inhabitants drink red or white with whatever they like, except for the most
special occasions and when the very finest wines are concerned.

Giving the When you give your order for the wine, should you be hesitant about trying
order to pronounce an unfamiliar name order it by its bin number alongside the
name on the wine list. Or if it is a wine from the waiter's native land, ask
him how you should pronounce it – that will charm him. As you become more
experienced, you will also want to ask about such details as who shipped the
Burgundy, or the producer of the German wine (ideally these should be given
on the wine list, but few wine lists are ideal) and, if two vintages are given
for a particular wine, you should ask which one is currently available.

The list should also always indicate whether a wine is bottled at the estate
where it was made or elsewhere – naturally the estate bottling will be more
expensive. If no vintage is indicated at the side of the name of a type of wine
which should have a date attached to it, then you must ask about this. Otherwise, and even in good faith, you may be charged for the wine of a fine or
great year, when what you have actually got is one from a much lighter and
possibly not as good a vintage. But these are all details which you can find

out about as you increase your experience of wine drinking (see Chapter 4).

Wine by the carafe   If you order wine by the carafe or half carafe, remember that, although in some restaurants you will get the contents of a bottle poured into a carafe, this is by no means invariable and usually it is understood that a carafe will hold slightly less than a bottle – possibly six glasses compared with the bottle's eight. And until legislation establishes some control of this, the only thing to do is to note the size of the glasses of wine that are sold by the glass and if in doubt, to ask the wine waiter how much a carafe or half carafe will serve. Sometimes there are small carafes that really only supply two glasses, but others may provide slightly more, and the waiter will know whether you should order the whole carafe or only a half, if you indicate how much you really want to drink.

How the wine should be served   When the wine comes, you should be shown the bottle. This is to check that you have got what you actually ordered, because it is very easy at a busy dispense, where the waiter goes to get the wine, for a different wine to be drawn from the bin in error.

Then the bottle should be opened in front of you. This, again, is to make sure that you get exactly what you have asked for. If you have asked for the wine to be decanted in advance, you should still have been shown the bottle

before it has been opened. The waiter may take it away to do the decanting, but again, ideally, he should do it at the side of your table.

A little wine is then poured into the glass of the host, who tastes it. Some people regard this as pretentious, but in fact it is wholly practical: should there be, by chance, any bits of cork still adhering to the inside of the bottle's neck, these will go into the host's glass and not spoil the look of the wine in the glass of guests. Also, the host can see both that the wine is of the right temperature and that it is in condition. It is only fair to say that sometimes this is not always immediately apparent and it is not unknown for the very occasional 'corked' bottle (*see Glossary*) to have been poured out after the host's approval, and only be eventually rejected when the definite smell with which corkiness is associated has made itself evident after a few minutes in the glass. But a badly-corked bottle or one that is thoroughly out of condition will have some kind of strange or obvious smell about it. Only when the host has approved the wine should the waiter then pour it for the other diners, serving the host last.

If, with a rather special wine, you feel inclined to ask the waiter to taste it as well, you should certainly do so, as this is one of the ways in which he will be able to increase his own knowledge of his craft. Don't worry – he should only pour a very small amount into a glass which he will take away to try, if he does not do so at the time you offer it.

Should you order another bottle of the same wine, either at the beginning of the meal or in the course of it, then it is absolutely *essential* to insist that you have a separate glass in which you taste the contents of the second bottle. With very fine wines a top-class establishment should, in fact, provide a separate glass for each diner with each bottle, even if the wine is nominally the same – although no two bottles of fine wine are ever exactly the same. The fact that one bottle is all right does not by any means imply that the second one will be in perfect condition also, and occasionally a wine waiter, who is anxious to serve, will rush around the table topping up glasses before the host can stop him and reject a 'corked' bottle – so that all the wine, good and bad, has therefore to be thrown away. If you have ordered your meal and your wines in advance and the wines are to be decanted, then although the wine waiter may show you a sample of the wines first, ideally he himself should have tasted it before your arrival and have passed it as in perfect condition.

If something is wrong Suppose there is something wrong with the wine. A dud bottle, even from the most impeccable of sources can appear in the finest of restaurants – it is one of the things that just happens. But, in fact, not half the many bottles that are rejected by customers really have anything wrong with them, and although the establishment should agree that, of course, you are right not to drink that particular wine, they may, in fact, use it up for their own suppers and say no more.

Before you reject a bottle as faulty, try to be sure that you are not doing so without due consideration: you may have had a lot of spirit-based cocktails before tasting the wine, and your palate will therefore be in rather an unbalanced state. You may find a wine quite strange to you, and reject it simply because you don't like it, which is quite different from its being out of condition. Or it may in fact just have been badly handled by an inexperienced wine waiter – cloudiness and deposits churned up in the wine, a cork inadequately extracted, glasses insufficiently rinsed from detergent and dried on smelly cloths, can all be reasons why people reject wines which in fact have nothing wrong with them at all. So think before you act.

And it is only fair, too, to give the wine a little chance to breathe and for you to both smell and taste it several times before you make up your mind definitely. Sometimes the small amount of air in the top of the bottle will result in a 'bottle stink' that is really unpleasant when the wine is first poured but which will soon disappear as the air gets at it. This is a reason, too, why it is ideal to draw the cork of a white wine some minutes before you are going to pour it, even if you then lightly replace this cork.

Of course, if you have already drunk all but about a quarter of the bottle, it is not fair then to send for the wine waiter, complain and expect the bottle to be replaced! (But people do this.).

The correct procedure, which need occasion no turmoil in the restaurant or agitation on your part, should you think that a particular bottle's contents are not as they should be, is to ask your guests' opinions and then, if they agree with you, to request them to stop drinking. Send for the wine waiter, ask for his opinion, saying that you are either disappointed in the wine or else that you think you detect something amiss. He should taste it with you and, as the customer is always right, he should then offer to replace it, but, as it is by no means unknown for two bottles in succession to be faulty, it is up to you to decide whether you want to try another bottle of the same wine (which of course may be very different indeed), or change the order altogether. In fact, perhaps the easiest way of telling whether a wine is out of condition in any way, whether you are trying it at home or in a restaurant, is to open another bottle of the same wine and compare the two – unless the second wine is also faulty, you will have no difficulty in deciding whether the first one is corked or not.

The management should replace the wine, not making any charge for the rejected bottle, and if they argue about this be quite firm that they should return it to their suppliers, who of course will replace it in their turn. The wine waiter may not have the authority to replace your bottle, but the manager certainly will, and he should be on hand if there is a suspicion of anything going wrong. Should there be any argument or demur on the part of the restaurant, avoid embarrassing your guests by further discussion of the matter, order something else, possibly a carafe wine, and say that you will make a written complaint to the suppliers. You should not be charged for the bottle you have rejected and if there is any fuss about this sort of situation, you are perfectly at liberty to refuse to pay any service charge or do any tipping. It takes courage to be prepared to do this kind of thing, but in the event it is surprising how the person who is calmly prepared to act in a practical and reasonable way has every advantage on his or her side.

Do you tip the wine waiter? If a wine waiter has given you special service of any kind, or if you are particularly pleased with his recommendations, then of course you can tip him separately if you wish, but it is by no means always expected that you will do so. Indeed, a smile at the outset, intelligent interest and polite consultation, with thanks expressed at the end, are often just as welcome. But from time to time you may like to thank friends among regularly-patronized catering staff.

Women in the chair In these days when women very often entertain men in restaurants, the question often arises – should the man, who is a guest, order the wine? In some people's view, it is both rude and inefficient if the woman asks him to do so; it indicates that she hasn't taken the trouble to try and learn enough about ordering the wine, as well as the food, and how does she know, anyway, that his opinion is likely to be of more value than hers? Even if she is entertaining someone whose experience in wine is vast, it is bound to be interesting to him to see what she chooses, and the trouble she takes to give her guest or guests pleasure is something that is always appreciated. An experienced wine waiter will be of the greatest help here, but if there is no one sufficiently expert available to be of assistance, a woman should still try and follow the procedures outlined earlier and, if necessary, ask the opinion of her guest – just as he might ask hers if he were doing the ordering – and then make up her own mind.

It is always possible, you should realize, for someone who is *really* knowledgeable about wine to help out the less experienced host or hostess, should he or she be likely to make a real mistake or choose something totally inappropriate, especially if there can be a few moments of conversation about possible choices. Reversing the more usual procedure, many women, who have enjoyed some experience of wine, would never think of taking over the ordering of this for the host, but it is always a simple matter to help someone inexperienced if they are in a difficulty, and one enjoys having a choice made in any event. If a man takes a woman out he, too, should know how to do it competently.

It is, perhaps, worth pointing out that, in many wine regions, there is nothing remarkable about the woman giving the orders for the wines as well as for the food in a restaurant if, in the opinion of her husband, she is more competent on this subject than he is; the happily married can perhaps discuss this and make up their own policies!

The look of the wine list   Quite a lot may be learned about a restaurant by simply looking at the wine list. In these days, many restaurants prefer to hand over responsibility of this to one particular source of supply, whether or not they are actually owned themselves by a chain of restaurants, which may supply all outlets from a central depot. There is nothing wrong with this, except that it can limit the range of wines available, even if the supplier is a merchant with wide resources, but it will mean that all the wines are chosen by people who have the same sort of buying policy. If the restaurant acts on its own as a buyer, then at least the composition of the list will be more individual, although not necessarily better. But usually it is better to have certain information included in the wine list, and when this is not there, you may very well conclude that either the restaurant does not care very much about its wines, or else the source of supply is possibly less reputable than it might be.

Obviously, no one would expect a range of fine French wines to be included on the list of an Italian restaurant, nor vice versa; however, customers can be unreasonable and unless the personality of the restaurateur is strong, the establishment may decide to play safe and list, say, a Chianti and an Asti, even if everything else is French. A good or first class and fairly large restaurant, of course, should have at least a moderate range of the classic wines of France, Germany, Italy and certain selected other countries or regions on its lists.

Details to watch for   In addition to the actual names of the wines, the good restaurant list, even if it is quite short, should also give the particulars about the growers or producers of any of the estate-bottled wines, particularly the finer German wines, and the Burgundy shippers; with the wines that are not estate bottled, the source of supply should be named and if you see the same names recurring here, then you will know that the particular establishment, who is the agent for all these wines, probably has the wine list in hand.

In a good or luxury restaurant, the wine waiter should know the source of supply of both the carafe wines and wines by the glass but, of course, in a humbler eating place, this is not always given and the source of supply may change frequently, which is not a bad thing at all.

Some restaurants attempt to show off in what seems unnecessary ways: for example, listing three or four different sorts of Liebfraumilch, several kinds of regional non-vintage wines such as St. Emilion, St. Julien, or Médoc on a single list, when it would be more interesting and not necessarily more expensive for the customer to have the option of trying at least one wine from a particular property; or they list several sorts of Champagne, at very high prices, when again it might be more helpful to the customer to offer a range of prices and styles of different sparkling wines.

Finally, but most important: whether you are looking at a long or short wine list and no matter what kind of restaurant you are eating in, the cheapest wine on the list should be the wine to order if in doubt. Not only will it be the least expensive if you are in for a disappointment, but it should be the wine which the manager drinks himself. Whether red or white, the cheapest wine should be the one by which the establishment is prepared to be judged, because it is quite easy to buy great wines, providing one has the money, but it takes skill and experience to select a good cheap one. Never be hesitant, therefore, about ordering the cheapest wine. Remember, also, that if the establishment finds a wine which they do not seem to be selling as fast as they would wish, they tend to put it second or, even more often, third up from the cheapest, because this is the one that the really nervous customer will order, not wishing to be thought mean by ordering the cheapest and not wanting to risk making an expensive mistake by having something higher up! So tend to avoid this one and, if you don't know anything about the other wines on the list, pick the cheapest one of all – which is what the experienced person will always do.

Chapter 9 *Spirits and Liqueurs*

Spirits are distillates. This means that they are distilled from alcoholic beverages of moderate or low strength so as to produce resulting liquids of high strength. The process is carried out by heating the original liquid so that it vapourizes and this vapour is cooled and condensed. Naturally, this is a very simplified explanation of a complicated procedure, which is varied according to the type of spirit involved.

The still that is used, as well as the ingredients and method of distillation, affect the character of the spirit. There are two main types of still; the patent or continuous still, which, as its name implies, operates continuously and which is used for grain whisky, gin and vodka. Then there is the pot still, in which the liquid is distilled in a big fat, onion-shaped container, usually made of copper, with a long spout coming out of the top. The fire whereby this is heated has to be most carefully controlled, and great skill is needed to ensure that the quality of the distillate is as it should be. Some spirits are distilled once, others twice, and a few as much as three times. The pot still is used for making Cognac, malt whisky, and certain types of rum. Sometimes the products of both pot still and continuous stills are combined.

Spirits are enjoyable and useful drinks and, both in the past and today, have proved their worth in many semi-medical applications. As they do not change once they go into bottle, the only care of them that is necessary in the home is to keep them standing upright, otherwise the spirit in the bottle tends to make the cork or stopper deteriorate. Because of their high alcoholic strength, too, they will not decline in quality for some time after the bottle is first opened, unlike wines. With very few exceptions, spirits are not sold with any vintage date attached to them, and the distribution of the best-known brands of the main types is virtually world-wide, so that to select them it is only really necessary to experiment and try a few different brands, decide which you like, and then you may be sure of getting it. It is worth while, however, to try the 'house brands' of any good wine merchant, store or liquor department, because, as such lines do not have to bear the weight of advertising, they may be good bargains as regards price and prove entirely satisfactory to the customer. Different brands of spirits vary, some of them enormously, and there are variations in strength as well but, within the same categories of style and strength, the differences between, say, types of blended Scotch or gin are not as wide as they would be between a similar range of wines. Spirits put out by the famous companies are all of high quality, and their production and labelling is strictly control- led; the fact that spirits are so heavily taxed makes them expensive com- modities, and if you are trying out different types in order to make up your mind which you like, it is usually possible to get a quarter bottle or even a miniature of the principal brands as a tester.

Brandy

Brandy, distilled from wine, may be made wherever wine is made and the brandies of different countries and regions will be individual and can be pleasant drinks.

Cognac, the supreme brandy of the world, comes from a specific region in the Charente district in the west of France. It is made only by the pot-still method and matured in oak casks, eventually being blended according to the style of the particular establishment responsible for it and to the type of brandy that it is wished to make: most Cognac houses will produce a brandy intended for using in mixed drinks, also one of slightly superior quality for drinking after meals or in a simple mix, and one of liqueur quality, which is meant to be drunk straight without being diluted. A number of illusions have grown up about aged Cognac, but although it is matured in cask it does not go on improving indefinitely if left there, and age is in itself not necessarily an asset. Once the Cognac goes into bottle it will virtually not change, so that there is no point whatsoever in paying vast sums for a cob- web-covered bottle reputed to be 'old' Cognac. If it was a young brandy of an unmatured and therefore harsh type when it went into the bottle, that is exactly what it will be like when it comes out! If it was an old brandy when it went into the bottle, then it will be an old brandy when you pour it out, but there is no need whatsoever for the bottle to be covered with dust and cobwebs.

By French law there are no vintages on Cognac nowadays, the great houses concentrating on maintaining the style of their various fine Cognacs. But sometimes a British merchant will ship a quantity of Cognac of a single year, which will be matured in the damp bonded warehouses of the British Isles; there it will mature slowly, the strength slightly declining and the character, when it is eventually bottled, being quite different from exactly the same Cognac matured in the dryer, warmer district of the Charente, in which, it is truly said, 'The sun is the best customer', because of the amount of brandy that evaporates from the casks – 10% annually.

PLATES 11 AND 12: *St. Emilion grapes* (right) *produce the great brandies of France, Cognac and Armagnac. Both wines are matured in oak casks, which help to give them their distinctive flavours: white oak from the forests of Limousin is used for Cognac, and local black oak for Armagnac.*

PLATES 13 AND 14: *A modern brandy distillery in Cognac* (left), *featuring the traditional pot still, which is usually of copper and shaped like an onion with a spout coming from the top.* (Below) *Pipes or casks of Bual wine maturing in a Madeira wine lodge.*

Armagnac is a brandy from the south-west of France, with a different flavour from Cognac. But it is also one of the great brandies of the world and has a rather gentle, subtle flavour – some people say that Armagnac is a feminine brandy, Cognac a masculine brandy. Many Armagnacs are bottled in a squat, flagon-shaped bottle, known as a *basquaise*.

Grape brandy, which is made in many parts of France and other wine-producing countries, is sometimes made by the pot still, other times by the continuous still, or may be a blend of the two types. It can be perfectly good for using in mixed drinks and there are superior types from various countries which can be enjoyed quite alone. Brandies from Spain, Italy, Greece, Cyprus, and virtually all the wine regions of the world can be pleasant drinks and are usually available in varying qualities, so that you can choose whether you use them in a mix or serve them as a liqueur. It is worth remembering, though, that the word *Cognac* in a variety of spellings is often used to signify brandy in general in countries other than France; the word is better known than brandy. But there is only one true Cognac and it is not fair to make comparisons of other brandies, however good, with it.

Whisky

Scotch whisky is always spelled as it is here. There are two types – malt and grain – and Scotch is only made in Scotland.

Malt whisky, which is distilled in a pot still and matured in oak casks, is made only from barley which has been 'malted' or allowed to sprout, afterwards being dried in a peat-fired kiln. The product of each distillery – there are about 117 working today – is a completely individual whisky, some of it being sold entirely for blending purposes, but other straight malts becoming increasingly widely known.

Grain whisky is made from unmalted barley and other cereals, and is produced in the patent or continuous still. All the well-known brands of Scotch are a blend of grain and malt, sometimes 40–50 different whiskies being used in a single blend; certain luxury whiskies, in which the proportion of malt is higher, or which are higher in strength, are also made.

Whiskey is always Irish. It is distilled in pot stills, but is rather different from the single malts of Scotland, and in general tends to be rather softer and possibly more fragrant than most Scotch.

Although Scotch is a unique product, excellent whiskies are also made in the New World, including **Bourbon**, made from grain and barley malt, and **Rye**, which must contain at least 51% rye grain. Bourbon, first made in Kentucky in the United States, is still only made in the U.S.A., but Rye is made both in the U.S.A. and Canada. These whiskies tend to be slightly lighter in style than Scotch, but it must not, therefore, be assumed that they are 'weaker' – they aren't!

Gin

Gin is distilled spirit rectified (which term means purified) and flavoured, sometimes from juniper, the French name for which, *genièvre*, gave the word 'gin' to the English language.

London gin, which is very dry, is world famous and put out by a number of establishments; **Plymouth gin**, made only by Coates of Plymouth, has a special flavour, tends to be a favourite with the Royal Navy, and is therefore often used for Pink gin, which is gin plus some drops of Angostura Aromatic Bitters. **Dutch, Hollands, Schiedam** or **Scandinavian gin**, or **Genever** (the Dutch word for juniper), is made in a pot still, unlike the London gins, and tends to be rather more definitely flavoured than the other type. It is also usually drunk alone, very cold.

Rum

Rum is the distillate of sugar cane, but does not in itself necessarily contain sugar or taste sweet. There are a variety of types, and in former times different parts of the West Indies were known for specifically different rums; today most of the rum-producing areas will make a range of rums. These include **white rum**, originally made in Cuba and a very popular spirit in the 1970's, ranging through the **light fragrant rums**, for which Martinique was at one time well known, the **darker type** (Demerara rum), formerly the speciality of Guyana, the **very dark, pungently-flavoured rums** in which Jamaica used to specialize, and the **dry light rums**, with which Barbados and Trinidad were associated. Rum can only legally be made where sugar cane is grown, which is why there is no English rum.

Vodka

Vodka is distilled either from grain spirit or molasses, and although it was originally Russian, some of the best vodka has since been made in Poland, and it is now produced in many countries, including Britain. Ordinary vodka, which can vary in strength, has very little if any flavour, but there are certain other vodkas flavoured with fruits, herbs, and other additives.

Liqueurs and apéritifs

There are literally hundreds of liqueurs and, as some may be drunk as apéritifs as well as after meals, it is quite difficult to know where to draw the line between a wine-based drink, such as Dubonnet or St. Raphaël, and the type of spirit formerly known only as a liqueur or post-prandial digestive, such as Cointreau or Crème de Menthe. In these more casual days, many drinks may be enjoyed at virtually any time, either before or after meals or quite outside the context of any food. A small number of the better known apéritifs and liqueurs are briefly described in the Glossary (*see pages* 186–196), but it should be remembered that liqueurs are usually based on spirits, and therefore are high in strength, and that some apéritifs, such as Lillet and Dubonnet, being wine-based, will deteriorate if the bottle is left open for any prolonged period.

Bitters

Bitters are as their name implies bitter. But they are valuable additives in many drinks and can also be extremely good as digestives, either neat or with soda or water.

Campari, bright pink and extremely refreshing as a long drink, is well known; **Fernet Branca**, which is brown and, to some people, has a very unpleasant strong herby taste, is famous as a pick-me-up, but it is also enjoyed by many people simply as a digestive, either before or after meals. Other similar drinks are **Ferro-China, Elixir,** and **Underberg Bitters. Angostura Aromatic Bitters**, which were evolved in the last century by a doctor, are intensely concentrated and are never drunk alone, but are added to various mixtures and can also be extremely useful in the kitchen (see Chapter 10). All bitters are expensive because of their high alcoholic content. But a little of any of them goes quite a long way.

Drinking spirits Brandy of all kinds, and the fine straight malt whiskies, have the most beautiful aroma, so that they should be drunk in glasses that enable this to be enjoyed. When either brandy or whisky is used in a mixed drink, or if it is to be diluted with water or soda, then the shape of the glass does not matter very much, but for the finest types of these spirits, a small globular glass is used; it should not be enormous – the goldfish-bowl brandy balloons merely dissipate the bouquet of the spirit before it can reach the nose of the drinker.

The ideal brandy glass is one that can be cupped in the palm of one hand – two hands if you have small palms. Such a glass should never be artificially heated as this, too, merely shocks the spirit which immediately releases its aroma before the drinker can come anywhere near it. The gentle warmth of the palm of the hand, coming through a fairly thin glass as the spirit is swirled around inside, will do the job better than anything else, and the use of the giant brandy balloon or the brandy warmer is something deplored by all who really know something about this beautiful spirit.

Fine brandy and whisky of all kinds are best diluted only by good spring water, but of course there is nothing to prevent you adding soda, ginger ale or anything else if you really wish. But tap water and ice cubes made from tap water in most towns is nowadays so chemically treated that it will blur the flavour of even the finest spirit. If you are treating guests to a luxury whisky of any kind, or to a fine brandy, it is courteous to have a bottle of still table water for adding to the drink.

Gin may be used in many mixes, and it is entirely a matter of personal taste as to how it is served. As has been mentioned above, the Dutch gins are usually taken in Holland, neat and iced. Vodka and schnapps of all kinds are, when they are drunk neat, also taken really iced – put the bottle in the freezer. An attractive way of serving them is to put the bottle into an empty can and fill this with water. Freeze and then remove the can, by dipping it into hot water. The 'jacket' of ice is ideal for keeping the drink cold. They should also be served in small glasses, as it is traditional when they are drunk alone to throw back the whole helping in one gulp – you are drinking this kind of spirit for the wonderful effect it has on you, not to sip and appraise the flavours.

Tequila, the Mexican spirit, which is also used in a number of cocktails, is also served iced when it is drunk alone; Ouzo, the Greek and Cypriot spirit, and similar white spirits made around the Mediterranean, are usually poured into a small glass, with or without ice, and then topped up with water according to the wishes of the drinker. **Pernod** (the south of France name for this drink is *pastis*) is also served diluted with water and, if liked, ice; and if you wish, you can drip a little water into it through a lump of sugar to sweeten the drink. But these are drinks which it is probably more fun to have in a bar or when one is travelling, rather than at home.

Rum is another spirit which can be served in a variety of ways, and there is no hard and fast rule or tradition about this, although white rum combines particularly happily with all types of citrus fruit juices.

In choosing soda, tonic, ginger ale or cola for diluting drinks, remember that the flavour of these can also vary considerably, and some are decidedly sweeter than others; try them neat first, as otherwise you may find that they change the character of a drink in a way that is not to your taste.

Most apéritifs and liqueurs should be served in moderately-sized glasses – not too small, as the majority of these drinks have a smell as well as a taste and if the glass is filled to the brim it is impossible to enjoy this. Smallish glasses are sensible simply because the drinks are usually strong. If they are used to make a long drink, of course, then it doesn't really matter about the glasses, which can be tall tumblers or big goblets.

The **fruit liqueurs,** such as **Cointreau** or the Basque liqueur, **Izarra,** can be very enjoyable when poured over ice cubes or crushed ice. But it should be remembered that when you add Campari or Bitters to another drink, it must then be stirred, because the spirit will not otherwise mix thoroughly with the other ingredients.

A touch that does greatly enhance the service of **white alcohols** or the true fruit brandies, such as **kirsch, framboise,** or **poire Williams** (which are not sweet at all, merely intensely fruity) is to chill the glasses in which you are going to serve the drink, either by putting them in the refrigerator, or swirling around a few ice cubes in them and then tipping these out. The chilling of the glass, which should be of a bulbous or tulip shape anyway, brings out the wonderful flavour of these fine spirits, although again, they are high in alcohol and only a little need be poured into each glass. Other liqueurs and apéritifs which are frequently served at room temperature are far more enjoyable if the bottles can be chilled, or the drinks poured over ice cubes – remember, the ice will melt and dilute the drink, so it is probably wise to pour a little more to each helping if you are going to serve them in this way.

Chapter 10 *Wines and Spirits in Cooking*

Wines and spirits can be a great asset in the kitchen, and very little need be used at a time. Indeed, in the household where wine is drunk once or twice a week, the 'heels' or remainder of the bottles will probably be quite enough for most culinary purposes. If you do have to buy wine for cooking, then it is not necessary to get anything special: go for something that is inexpensive, but not necessarily harsh and, as far as white wine is concerned, nothing too sweet. Some merchants do provide cooking wine at a low cost. Keep red and white wines separate, and use half bottles rather than whole bottles for this, so that the exposure of the wine to the air inside the bottle is kept to a minimum; drainings of wine will keep like this for several weeks, and dregs of port, sherry and brandy, as well as vermouth, can be added as well. Spirits should be kept apart. Sometimes gin and other spirits can be employed in cooking to advantage, but in general their use is occasional.

A recipe will usually specify whether red or white wine is to be used but, as you experiment, you will find that it is perfectly possible to incorporate a spoonful or two of wine in many dishes to their great advantage. By the way, don't be frightened that the use of wine in any recipe makes it unfit for children or young people to eat because, if the recipe incorporating the wine specifies long cooking, all trace of the alcohol will be driven off within a few minutes anyway, and only the flavouring of the wine will remain. And it is also better to use too little rather than too much – sometimes people are extravagant with wines and spirits in special dishes, but in fact nothing should ever have a pronounced flavour of any wine, except possibly a trifle. If you double the quantities of whatever wine or spirit the recipe specifies, you will alter the proportions and may in fact be thoroughly disappointed with the result.

Very often you will find that you can make use of the wine that you are going to drink with a meal in the recipe that you are preparing. This simplifies everything and, with red wine, you can simply decant the wine and use the small amount remaining in the bottom of the bottle. But it is not necessary to match wines with food exactly; for example, you can do a stew, such as coq au vin, which is essentially a Burgundian recipe, and make use of a little claret, Spanish or other red wine if this is what you happen to have. The only thing is that the recipe will be slightly altered if the wine is different. You would not, of course, use even a medium sweet white wine in what should be a succulent stew or rich gravy, for which red wine is always more suitable. And if you are making a delicate pale-coloured sauce, then a dry white wine, or half the quantity of vermouth are the ideal additives, as a red wine will spoil the colour. If you are substituting wine for stock or adding it to stock, which is sometimes helpful, then it is worthwhile to bear in mind the ultimate colour of the dish you are cooking – is it going to be cream or darkish brown?

Sauces and gravies   The simplest sauce can be made merely by pouring a tablespoon or so of wine into the roasting tin or skillet after you have removed the meat and drained off any surplus fat, and just stirring all the juices and the wine together, before reducing the whole slightly. If you are adding cream to a sauce of this kind, remember to turn the heat down and add the cream very gradually, so that it does not curdle. You should always reduce the wine and dissipate the alcohol in it by rapid boiling in making sauces and gravies in this way.

To baste meat or poultry with wine also results in an excellent gravy. You simply boil up a glass of red or white wine with two to three shallots, plus a little garlic, if you like the flavour, or simply use onions, and flavour the whole with freshly-ground black pepper and a little salt. Reduce this by fast boiling to about half the original quantity and then pour it over the meat.

Wine or brandy can be used to moisten and enrich the stuffings for meat or poultry, although be very careful not to overdo this. For jugging hare, and for certain recipes involving long cooking of kidneys, the use of port or Madeira is traditional, but generally fortified wines should be used with some caution, as they can be both assertive in flavour and slightly sweet. But you can use this type of wine for baking apples, or when you are stewing apples and other fruit, and sweet sherry as well as Marsala can be used in trifles, syllabubs and zabaglione, which can also all be made with a sweet table wine, such as a Sauternes, as a change.

A small glass of wine is a useful addition to any court bouillon in which you are going to poach meat, fish or poultry. There is a famous recipe for poaching salmon in red wine (Saumon Chambord), and this can be delicious, but in general a dryish white wine is used in a court bouillon of this kind for fish.

Soups   A little fortified wine, particularly sherry but port as well, can be added to certain types of soup, and on such occasions the wine need only be added while the soup is being heated up immediately before being served. It is very important not to add too much – as a well-known member of the sherry trade once said, 'If I can taste the sherry in the soup, there is too much.' For most cream soups, including bisques and game soups, a generous tablespoonful or a very small wine glass is sufficient wine for four to six people. Brandy is also a good addition to a bisque, and you can put a glass of port, claret or other red wine in a meat soup.

Marinades   Wine may be used as a marinade for meat or fish, and can both tenderize and enhance the flavour. A simple marinade is made by mixing together a small glass of wine with rather less oil, and spooning this over whatever is to be marinated, as it lies in a dish, together with a bouquet garni, a few peppercorns and a small sliced onion. The food can either be later roasted in the marinade itself, or else the marinade can be rinsed off and possibly reduced to use as a baste. It can give a wonderful gamey flavour to cuts that are otherwise lacking in taste.

Brandy,   All these spirits can be used to advantage in the kitchen. Possibly their
whisky and   best known role is that of setting light to the Christmas pudding, but fruit
rum   such as bananas, peaches, slices of pineapple and cherries can also be flamed. The spirit should be slightly warmed beforehand and the spoon in which it is to be ladled over the pudding or fruit should also be hot.

If you have cooked something, whether it is meat or fish, in a small pan or skillet, then a delicious additional flavour can be added and any grease removed by a final flaming of the food in spirit when the cooking is finished. The action of setting the sauce in the pan alight and spooning this all over the food will get rid of any excess fat. Simply heat whatever spirit is to be used in a ladle or small pan, set light to it – a taper is probably easier to use than a match, which you may drop into the pan itself – and pour the flaming spirit over the food, continuing to scoop it up and stir it around until all the flames have died out. Pancakes can also be flamed in this way, but for them and for other sweet dishes, kirsch, the cherry liqueur, or Cointreau or Grand Marnier, orange-flavoured liqueurs, may be substituted for plain brandy.

A little brandy, whisky or rum can be very helpful when you are making both pâtés and rich fruit cakes and puddings. Frankly, it is rather a waste to add the spirit to any mixture to be cooked for a long time, but when the dish is ready you can pierce it in several places with a needle or thin skewer and drip in a small quantity of spirit. During the time that any pâté or cake is kept the spirit will spread and impregnate the whole with a wonderful smell, and it will, in fact, act as a preservative. But again, you only need to use a very little. Cold mousses and fruit jellies can similarly be enhanced by the addition of a little liqueur of a suitable flavour just before they are put to set.

Fruit liqueurs may be used in very small quantities to improve whipped cream, and of course they may be added to fruit salads and trifles, but many people make the mistake of using either too much liqueur, which results in a very pronounced taste not liked by everyone, or else too many different kinds; the latter, when thrown together without great discrimination and previous experimentation, usually result in a rather unpleasant and unharmonious taste. The orange-flavoured liqueurs are generally the most useful in the kitchen and the cherry liqueurs are very useful too. Any chocolate liqueur may be used with a filling for meringues or to garnish ice cream; generally a miniature of any liqueur will be quite sufficient for a dinner party when the spirit is to be used in this way.

Some other ideas   The herby liqueurs should be used with great caution in the kitchen, as their flavour is usually too pronounced to combine well with food, but Green Chartreuse or Strega can be poured over a plain vanilla ice cream, and certain of the herb liqueurs may also be added to savoury dips. Angostura Aromatic Bitters are extremely useful, and their spicy fresh flavour enhances sandwich spreads and savoury butters, and can also improve salad dressings and certain sauces.

The use of wine or spirits in any form of cooking is something that can really be learned only by experimentation, but the 'certain something' that even a few drops of wine can give to a recipe should be quite sufficient to personalize this dish as your very own speciality. Remember, that you must distinguish between the sort of flavour that an addition of this kind can give to a dish that is going to be cooked for a long time and with which the wine or spirit should thoroughly amalgamate, and the kind of food to which the wine or spirit is added only at the last minute, such as in the flambé pan, or in which the food is not going to be cooked at all. But when in doubt – use only a *very* little. It is always possible to add more; it is never easy to counteract too much.

Glossary of Terms and Names

Abbocato Italian descriptive term, which usually implies that wines so labelled are slightly sweet or even fairly sweet.

Advocaat Made from egg yolks and either spirits or wine, low in alcoholic strength, this drink is made both in Holland and the U.K. and can be drunk at any time, although probably not before any fine wines are to be served.

Alcool blanc Any drink in this category is a fruit brandy, kept in glass, not wood, so that it remains pure white. Usually such spirits are simply distilled from the fruit and not sweetened, and are markedly fruity. The famous types are kirsch (cherry) and framboise (raspberry). They should ideally be served chilled.

Amabile See Abbocato.

Anis, anisette Many liqueurs are made with this flavour, and it also is used for apéritifs, of which Pernod and pastis are possibly the most famous. As might be expected, if you don't like aniseed, you won't like this type of drink.

Aquavit or schnapps Spirits produced in northern countries, usually made from grain spirit flavoured with caraway. They should be served iced, are tossed off, not sipped, and are never taken without something to eat as well.

B.O.B. 'Buyer's Own Brand' is a term often used for a Champagne bought specially for a particular merchant and bearing his label. Can be excellent value, as it will not have to bear the weight of the advertising of the *grandes marques*.

Bénédictine This herby liqueur was first made by Dom Bernardo Vincelli, in 1510 at the Bénédictine abbey near Fécamp in Normandy. The abbey was destroyed in the French Revolution, but the recipe was kept and eventually was made again at what is now an impressive distillery and museum. B. and B. is Bénédictine and brandy.

Blanc de blancs Literally 'white from whites' – i.e. a wine made solely from white grapes. Often used in connection with Champagne, but this term can be applied to other wines, both still and sparkling.

Blend Unless wines are made from single vinestocks, it simply is not possible to produce a wine that is not blended, and therefore the use of the term in a critical sense is merely silly and shows ignorance. Wines of the finest kinds are made from blends of grapes, from blends of vattings, from blends of vintages and from blends of plots within the vineyards. The blender's work is, rightly, described as an art.

Bodega Spanish term for almost any place where wine is kept but in particular the lofty, above-ground cellars of the sherry shippers in the sherry region.

Body This term describes the weight of a wine in the mouth, due mainly to its alcoholic content as well as other physical components. It varies with the quality, style and origin of a wine.

Bourgeois growth Term relating to red Bordeaux wines of increasing importance, as these smaller-scale wines or growths, now being made with contemporary skills, are both good value and of great interest to the wine lover, especially for everyday purposes, in view of the high prices of the classed growths.

Breeding A quality of flavour and texture in good wine due to the renown of the vineyard, the grapes, and the winemaker.

Brut Pronounced 'brute', this term, often applied to Champagne, implies that the wine has had no additional sweetening and is, therefore, very dry.

Byrrh French wine-based apéritif, made in the Roussillon region; it is sweetish with a flavour of quinine.

Cabernet The Cabernet sauvignon and the Cabernet franc are two of the great red wine grapes of the world. They are two of the claret grapes, and the Cabernet franc also makes the fine red wines of the Loire, and the best Loire rosé.

Calisay Sweetish herby liqueur from Spain.

Calvados Apple brandy from Normandy. Roughly the same as the American applejack.

Cap Corse Corsican wine-based apéritif; it is slightly sweet.

Chai Term used in the Bordeaux region for the wine store which, because of the nature of the soil, can seldom be under the ground.

Chartreuse A digestive liqueur, named after the Charterhouse (Chartreuse) founded near Grenoble by St. Bruno in 1084. It became famous in the 19th century, when some French army officers were billeted in the monastery. The Carthusians were expelled from France in 1903, and made their liqueur in Spain until 1931, when they returned. Both green and yellow types of the herby liqueur are made, in a very modern distillery at Voiron, the yellow being slightly less alcoholic than the green, which is one of the strongest liqueurs made.

Claret The common name for red Bordeaux wine, derived from the old French, *clairette*.

Classification This term usually means the wines of the different regions of Bordeaux and, in particular, those of the Médoc, which were classified in 1855. They are not, however, classified according to merit but all of them should be at least good, and most of them are fine wines.

Corked wine Describes an unpleasant smell of the cork and a mouldy taste in the wine due to a diseased cork.

Cosecha Spanish word meaning 'harvest', hence indicating a vintage date on a label.

Crémant French term literally meaning 'creaming' and describes certain slightly sparkling wines.

Dock glass: Shaped like an elongated tulip or sherry *copita*, and used for sampling or critically tasting wines.

Drambuie Name taken from Gaelic words, signifying 'the drink that satisfies', this is a whisky-based liqueur, the recipe for which was given by Bonnie Prince Charlie to Mackinnon of Strathaird, who helped him escape after Culloden. The formula is still the secret of the Mackinnon family.

Dubonnet French wine-based apéritif, available in two types, Dubonnet Blonde being gold and rather dryer than the pinkish-red type.

Fernet Branca One of the most famous of bitters, admirable as a digestive or pick-me-up. Other well-known brands are Ferro China, Martini's Elixir, and Underberg.

Fine Pronounced 'feen', this is brandy distilled from wine – not necessarily Cognac, although in a good restaurant it should be.

Fior d'Alpi Italian liqueur, usually in tall bottles containing twigs with lumps of crystallized sugar on them. It is fairly pungent and digestive.

First growths By these are invariably signified the great first growths picked out in the Bordeaux classification of the wines of the Médoc and

Graves in 1855. One red Graves only was included – Château Haut Brion. The others are: Château Margaux in the parish of Margaux, Châteaux Lafite and Latour and, since 1973, Château Mouton-Rothschild, all of them in the parish of Pauillac. These wines are invariably expensive, and nowadays all are château-bottled. Latour puts that it is a first growth on its label, Lafite never has.

Flor The curious covering of yeast that 'flowers' at certain times on the surface of the fino sherries in cask.

Frizzante Italian term implying that a wine is slightly sparkling.

Gay Lussac Man who gave his name to the system of measuring the strength of drinks by expressing them in terms of percentage of alcohol by volume – usually the easiest for people to understand.

Gentian Category of rather bitter apéritifs, of which Suze, bright yellow, is probably the best known. Admirable digestives.

Glayva Herb and spice liqueur, based on whisky.

Glen Mist Whisky-based liqueur, incorporating herbs, spices and honey.

Grande Marque A *vin de marque* is a branded wine. In the Champagne region some of the most famous establishments form the association of *Grandes Marques*, but excellent Champagne is also made by houses outside this association.

Grappa Italian spirit distilled from the residue of grapes left over after the final pressing for wine. It is usually colourless and strong.

Grenadine Pinkish, sweetish flavouring for drinks – non-alcoholic usually, but sometimes it does contain a very little alcohol.

Guignolet Type of cherry brandy.

Hectare Metric measure of area, abbreviated to ha. It is equivalent to 10,000 square metres or 2.471 acres.

Hectolitre Liquid measure used in France, abbreviated to hl. in writing and 'hecto' in speech. It is equivalent to 100 litres or 21·9976 gallons.

Hock Derived from the German town Hochheim, the word has come to denote any Rhenish or Rhine wine.

Hospices de Beaune The old peoples' home and hospital in Beaune in Burgundy, supported by the sales of wines from the vineyards with which it has been endowed since the 15th century. The wines all come from the Beaune region and the annual sale, attended by buyers from all over the world, is the occasion for many celebrations. Each wine bears the name of the original donor.

Irish Mist Liqueur based on Irish whiskey, herbs and honey.

Izarra Green and yellow herby liqueurs, based on Armagnac, made in the south-west of France. The green is slightly stronger than the yellow. The name is the Basque word for 'star'.

Kahlúa A coffee liqueur.

Kümmel Pronounced 'kimmel', this is a caraway-flavoured liqueur. The oldest type was first made by the firm of Lucas Bols in Amsterdam in 1575.

Liebfraumilch German wine of a style specially created for export markets – it is seldom seen in Germany. It probably originally got its name from the wines of the Church of Our Lady at Worms, where there is a vineyard adjoining the church, but these wines (of the Liebfrauenstift) are now nothing to do with Liebfraumilch. It is a wine of a certain quality, which may or may not bear a vintage label, which many of the German wine houses produce, usually from the wines of the Rheinhessen region; sparkling types are also made.

Lindisfarne Whisky-based, British honey liqueur.

Liqueur d'Or French liqueur made by Garnier, containing flakes of gold. Danziger Goldwasser is another liqueur of the same type.

Liqueur wines Nothing to do with liqueurs, this is the E.E.C. term used officially for fortified wines, such as port and sherry,

Lodge Wine store in Portugal, particularly in the port region.

Maderised White wines which have darkened in colour due to the air are thought to resemble Madeira – hence 'maderised'.

Maraschino Liqueur made from the distillate of fermented maraschino cherries.

Marc Pronounced 'mar', this is the spirit distilled from the mass of pressed grapes after the juice has been extracted for wine-making. It is usually strong.

Mis en bouteille . . . Term used to indicate where, in France, the wine has been bottled. All-important is where: *au château, au domaine, à la propriété* all mean estate bottling. If a place is given, such as Bordeaux or Beaune, this can indicate that the shipper has bottled the wine in his premises there; the wine will not have been moved far from where it was made. But information such as this should be definite and associated with a reputable and well-known establishment. British bottling of wines can be first-rate and certainly better than any doubtful foreign bottling.

Moelleux French term meaning 'like bone marrow' and, therefore, concentrated. It is often used to denote a sweet wine.

Mousseux French term meaning fully sparkling.

Mouton Cadet Evolved during the depression of the mid-thirties, this claret is now possibly the biggest-selling wine of its kind in the world. It is made at Mouton Rothschild, but it should be stressed that, although some of the wine comes from the Mouton vineyards (which include Mouton Baron Philippe, another classed growth), Mouton Cadet, which bears a vintage date and has had at least two years ageing in bottle before it is sold in the U.K., must never be confused with the great first growth, Mouton-Rothschild. Mouton Cadet now bears the A.O.C. *Bordeaux* and the wines which go towards making it up may come from anywhere in the Bordeaux region. Mouton Rothschild and Mouton Baron Philippe are very great Pauillac wines indeed – and very expensive. Mouton Cadet can never be more than a good red Bordeaux.

Muscat One of the well-known wine grapes of the world; it can make both dry and sweet wines; they invariably have a pronounced fragrance, which can reasonably be described as 'grapey'.

Must Grape juice before it has been turned into wine by the process of fermentation.

Négociant French term meaning 'shipper', which is used in particular in Burgundy and Bordeaux.

Noble rot *Pourriture noble* in French, *edelfäul* in German, this is the action of a type of fungus on the grapes, which causes them to shrivel and concentrates the juice. It is especially peculiar to the great German wine regions and the Sauternes area of Bordeaux, and is not to be confused with other types of rot that may affect a vineyard. The wines made from grapes acted on by this fungus are very luscious and fragrant.

Nobility The ultimate in a wine when all its qualities, such as body, bouquet, flavour and maturity, reach their peaks in perfect harmony.

Noyau Liqueur made from peach and apricot kernels.

Oenology Study or knowledge of wine.

Orange Curaçao Liqueurs, which can also be served as apéritifs, based on the peel of bitter oranges, originally from the Island of Curaçao. Triple sec is a type of Curaçao, and Cointreau is possibly the most famous. Grand Marnier is an orange liqueur based on Cognac. Curaçao can be made in various colours and there is one that is bright blue.

Ouzo Aniseed-flavoured apéritif or liqueur, made in the Mediterranean countries. It is usually drunk chilled, plus water.

Passe-Tout-Grains Red Burgundy made from a mixture of the Pinot noir grapes (which make the finest red Burgundies) and the Gamay (which is the grape of the Beaujolais).

Pastis South of France general name for aniseed drinks (Pernod is made near Pontarlier in the north-east), of which Berger and Ricard are well-known brands. Usually served with ice and water, sometimes the water being dripped in through a lump of sugar. Originally Pernod contained absinthe, but this cannot legally be used now in France because of the narcotic content. It is still, however, a strong drink.

Perlant French term meaning very slightly sparkling or something like a 'prickle'.

Pétillant French term meaning lightly sparkling.

Pimm's Evolved by James Pimm at his oyster bar in the City of London in 1841. The formula is still a guarded secret. Until recently, six different Pimm's were available, with different spirit bases, but now 'the original gin sling' is the only one made. The drink can be short or long, diluted with fizzy lemonade or, for very special occasions, sparkling wine or even Champagne.

Pineau des Charentes Apéritif of the Charente region of France, consisting of grape juice and Cognac.

Pinot The family of grapes producing some of the world's finest wines, both red and white.

Pisco Type of brandy distilled from Muscat wine in many South American countries, and notably Peru.

Poire Williams One of the most distinctive types of *alcool blanc*, made by distilling William pears.

Ponche Soto Brownish Spanish liqueur, in a silver bottle.

Porrón The vessel, like a triangular flask with a spout, used often for wine in Spain. It can pour into the mouth of the drinker, hence was a useful wine container if glasses were in short supply. It originates from the wineskin, carried on horseback, from which a thin stream of wine could be directed into the mouth of a number of people, without anyone having to put their mouth up against the skin.

Poteen, potheen The word means 'little pot', and signifies illegally-distilled Irish whiskey.

Preiserbeerlikoer German cranberry liqueur.

Punt The hollow at the base of some wine bottles, in which any deposit can accumulate.

Putt, puttonyos Measure, used to indicate the amount of sweetness in Hungarian Tokay – the more *putts*, the sweeter the wine.

Quinta Portuguese word for 'estate'. Certain very fine ports are single estate wines, Quinta do Noval and Quinto do Roeda being famous ones.

Rasteau Sweetish, slightly fortified wine made at the bottom of the Rhône valley in France.

Ratafia Many ratafias were once made, but now it is usually only found in Champagne, where it is generally slightly sweet. The name comes from the drink taken on the signing of a legal document, after which the notary pronounced the words, 'Ut rata fiat' – that is, 'May it be ratified'.

Retsina Greek resinated wine – you either like it or loathe it. White or rosé, it should always be served chilled.

Riesling The first syllable is pronounced to rhyme with 'geese', not 'rice'. One of the great, even possibly the greatest, white wine grapes of the world, it makes all the finest German wines and, in its different varieties, enormous quantities of fresh, dryish white wines in many countries.

Riserva Term applied to certain Italian wines of quality, usually indicating longer than usual maturation in cask.

Rosé Wine made pink either by blending red and white wines, or by allowing the skins of black grapes to remain in the must just long enough to tinge it. It is usually light in style, but some southern rosés are fuller in character. Pleasant, but it is by no means a 'when in doubt' wine.

Royal Mint-Chocolate Liqueur evolved by Peter Hallgarten in recent years, which exactly captures the flavour of bitter chocolate and bitter mint.

Sabra Israeli liqueur, made from bitter oranges and bitter chocolate.

Sapindor French herby liqueur, put up in a bottle that resembles a piece of tree-trunk.

Sauvignon blanc One of the world's great white wine grapes; it is especially famous as one of the grapes that make Sauternes, and, now used alone, many other dry white Bordeaux, as well as some of the finest wines of the

Loire, including Sancerre. The local name for it at Pouilly-sur-Loire is Blanc Fumé.

Schaumwein German term for sparkling wine.

Sekt German term used for German sparkling wine.

Sémillon One of the great white wine grapes of the world, famous for being one of the grapes making the fine Sauternes.

Southern Comfort American liqueur, based on Bourbon whiskey and flavoured with oranges and peaches.

Spritzig German term used to describe a wine which is 'lively' or has a very slightly 'prickly' taste, sometimes even having a very slight sparkle. The French term is *pétillant*. Some of the finest white wines display this trait when they are young, and the Portuguese vinhos verdes are made so as to be *pétillant*.

Strega Yellow Italian liqueur. If you share Strega with anyone, says the legend, you will always love them!

Sur lie Literally 'on the lees', a French term signifying that the wine has not been removed from any deposit in the cask before being bottled. It may therefore possess a special freshness and is sometimes *pétillant*. The term is most often used in connection with Muscadet.

Swedish Punsch A type of Batavian rum, sometimes diluted with hot water, but definitely a strong drink.

Sylvaner World-famous white wine grape, making very fresh wines. Usually spelt Silvaner when referring to those in Germany.

Tannin A natural substance found in grape skins which is extracted during fermentation; it is essential to red wines for long life. Too much tannin, as is quite common at first in young red wines, dries the roof of the mouth and tongue, similar to the effect raw rhubarb has.

Tequila Mexican spirit, made from the fermented hearts of the maguey plant. It should, traditionally, be knocked back after you have put a little salt on your hand and licked it off and then had a few drops of fresh lime or lemon juice. It is also used in many cocktails, of which the best-known is probably the Marguerita.

Tia Maria A very popular coffee liqueur.

Toni Kola Nothing to do with cola the fizzy drink, this is a type of French bitters.

Trappistine French herb liqueur.

Trou Normand Brand name for a type of Calvados. But the *trou Normand* is also the portion of Calvados served in the middle of one of the gigantic Norman banquets, by way of digestive and as an encouragement to go on eating.

Ullage The space between the cork and the level of the wine in a bottle, or between the bung and the level of wine in a cask.

Varietal American term signifying the variety of grape.

Velenche or pipette The type of siphon used to draw samples of wine from the cask in France.

Vendange French term for the harvesting of the grapes. See also **Vintage**.

Vendemmia Italian term for the harvesting of the grapes. See also **Vintage**.

Venencia The silver cup on a pliable whalebone handle, used for drawing samples from the sherry butt.

Verveine du Vélay French herb liqueur.

Vieille Cure French herb liqueur, based on both Armagnac and Cognac.

Vin de consommation courante Wine for everyday drinking.

Vin de garde Literally 'wine to keep' – that is, worth keeping.

Vin d'honneur A fairly formal drink, usually Champagne.

Vin de marque Branded wine.

Vin de presse Usually signifies wine made after the first pressing – that is, not so good, and probably kept for local consumption.

Vin de la région This is the phrase to use when you want a local wine. Vin de pays has rather a contemptuous significance – possibly something ever so ordinary.

Vin de tête Wine made from the first or one of the first pressings – therefore of extra quality.

Vinho verde Pronounced 'veenyo vaird', Portuguese wine, which is 'green' only in the sense that it is young. It is dry and with a very slight sparkle. There is red made as well as white – but no rosé is a vinho verde.

Vino de pasto Spanish term for wine with a meal – and in the sherry region they will drink sherry throughout, which is why some sherries have this term on their labels.

Vintage Harvest time when the grapes are gathered to make wine. In the northern hemisphere this takes place from about mid-September onwards, the more northern vineyards starting later, and those in Germany sometimes continuing to vintage until Christmas or the first heavy frosts. The term 'a vintage wine' is one used to imply that the wine may benefit by some maturation. Wines which do not bear a vintage date, and many of those that do – such as Muscadet – are intended to be drunk young and fresh and any date serves only to indicate that they are still young. The insistence of many of the public on wines having vintage labels is both silly and, sometimes, a temptation to the unscrupulous simply to stick on any vintage date. Age is not by any means an advantage, and the bulk of the wines made and enjoyed throughout the world are – rightly – non-vintage. Even the finest vintage wine only has a limited life, this varying according to the style of wine and the particular vintage, so that general insistence on having vintage wines merely indicates an ill-informed drinker.

Wine fraternities The most famous of these is probably the Chevaliers du Tastevin in Burgundy, formed to publicize the wines during the depression of the 1930's. There are now numerous fraternities in many countries and wine regions, and their picturesque ceremonies and work in publicity and tourism are most agreeable and effective. Usually, but not invariably, the officials of these orders are persons of importance in the production of the wine or spirit (and sometimes cheese) concerned. Although membership of any wine order is an honour, it can sometimes be bought, and someone who belongs to a wine order should not be assumed to be an authority on that particular wine – they may just be a grateful drinker of it.

Zinfandel Red wine grape, possibly native to America, used extensively in California.

Zwicker Term used to denote a blend of Alsatian wines from different grapes (they are usually made from a single grape). **Edelzwicker** denotes that the grapes used are of 'noble' varieties.

Bibliography

A Wine Primer by André Simon (Penguin, 1973)

The Penguin Book of Wines by Allan Sichel (Penguin, 1971)

Wines and Spirits by L. W. Marrison (Penguin, 1973)

Wines and Spirits by Alec Waugh and the Editors of TIME-LIFE BOOKS (revised 1971 by Time Inc.)

Wines and Spirits of the World edited by Alec Gold (Virtue, 1972)

The World Atlas of Wine by Hugh Johnson (Mitchell Beazley, 1971)

Wine by R. S. Don, M.W. (English Universities Press 1969)

Off The Shelf, Gilbey Vintners' Guide to Wines and Spirits (revised edition, 1972)

The Book of Drinking by John Doxat (Paul Hamlyn, 1973)

The Wines of Burgundy by H. W. Yoxall (Penguin, 1974)

The Wines of Bordeaux by Edmund Penning-Rowsell (Penguin, 1973)

The Wines of Central & South-eastern Europe by R. E. H. Gunyon (Duckworth, 1971)

The Wines of Italy by Cyril Ray (Penguin, 1971)

The Wines of Spain and Portugal by Jan Read (Faber & Faber, 1973)

Champagne by Patrick Forbes (Gollancz, 1967)

Sherry by Julian Jeffs (Faber & Faber, revised edition, 1970)

Cognac by Cyril Ray (Peter Davies Ltd., 1973)

Liqueurs by Peter Hallgarten (Wine & Spirit Publications, 1967)

Wine Tasting by J. M. Broadbent, M.W. (Christie Wine Publications, 1973)

Index